Christ the Stranger: The Theology of Rowan Williams

Benjamin Myers

D1494406

t&t clark

Published by T&T Clark International

A Continuum Imprint

The Tower Building	80 Maiden Lane
11 York Road	Suite 704
London	New York
SE1 7NX	NY 10038

www.continuumbooks.com

Benjamin Myers has asserted his right under the Copyright, Designs and Patents Act, 1988, to be identified as the Author of this work.

Rowan Williams' poetry used by kind permission of The Perpetua Press, Oxford.

Chapter 5 is adapted from Benjamin Myers, 'Disruptive History: Rowan Williams on Heresy and Orthodoxy,' in *On Rowan Williams: Critical Essays*, ed. Matheson Russell (Eugene: Cascade, 2009). Used by permission of Wipf & Stock Publishers, www.wipfandstock.com.

Piero della Francesca's *Resurrection* used by permission of akg-images/Electa.

Christ Pantocrator mosaic used compliments of The Yorck Project, DirectMedia/ Wikipedia.

Our Lady of Vladimir and Rublev's icon of the Trinity used compliments of St Isaac of Syria Skete, www.skete.com.

British Library Cataloguing-in-Publication Data
A catalogue record for this book is available from the British Library.

ISBN: HB: 978-0-567-56236-4
PB: 978-0-567-59971-1

Typeset by Deanta Global Publishing Services, Chennai, India
Printed and bound in Great Britain

To my mother and father

CONTENTS

Nah ist
Und schwer zu fassen der Gott.
The god is near and hard to grasp.

—Friedrich Hölderlin

PREFACE

Writing a book about Rowan Williams is a bit like riding a bicycle into the library: you know you probably won't get away with it, but it's exhilarating while it lasts. Williams is one of the most subtle and complex Christian intellectuals of our time. Restless and versatile, his writing moves back and forth across traditions, disciplines, genres, and idioms. History and philosophy, theology and spirituality, translation and poetry, aesthetics and literary criticism: his tastes and his curiosities are as catholic as his theology. And his sources and influences are wildly diverse: Anglo-Catholicism and Welsh Nonconformity, Augustine and Hegel, Freud and Wittgenstein, Vladimir Lossky and Sergius Bulgakov, Donald MacKinnon and Iris Murdoch, T. S. Eliot and Gillian Rose. These are not names that one normally meets in such close proximity, and their uneasy juxtaposition generates much of the peculiar energy of Williams' thought. It is this teeming diversity, the surprising elasticity of his imagination, that most intrigues me. The pages that follow are no more than a record of my curiosity, my fascination with the way Williams thinks and writes and reads. In this book, I hope to give some impression of the expansiveness of Williams' work and to show that his complexity is sustained by a deeper unity of vision: a vision of Jesus Christ as an intimate stranger, crucified and rising up into the broken world of human experience.

Williams is a catholic thinker. The scope of his observation, and the genres and idioms in which he works, bear witness to the universal scope – the catholicity – of the gospel. That is why his writing, from psychology and church history to poetry and literary criticism, is always gently, persistently *theological*. A study of fourth-century Latin heresy or the interpretation of a Russian novel can become a spiritual exercise once it is understood as a partial yet real reflection of Christ, the one whose risen life is catholic and unbounded.

This accounts for much of the complexity of Williams' thought. His imagination is a room arranged with pieces from different places and periods. Ancient and modern, eastern and western, sit side by side in a colourful and provocative mélange, drawing the eye to novel and unexpected objects, never allowing it to rest on any one item. Yet his work is no mere bricolage of curiosities. What holds it together is a conviction that Christ is universally available, that the truth of the gospel can be refracted through all the disparate fragments of human experience and tradition.

You could, I think, hardly find a better description of Williams' thought than his own remark on Thomas Merton, written in 1978:

> Merton's genius was largely that he was a massively unoriginal man; he is extraordinary because he is so dramatically absorbed by every environment he finds himself in . . . . All these influences flow into one constant place, a will and imagination turned Godward.[1]

At a time when tradition is widely ignored and intellectual novelty is prized as an end in itself, Williams' uniqueness lies in this sort of 'massive unoriginality,' the expansive catholicity of a baptized imagination.

In this book, I will offer an account of Williams' development and of the sources and ideas that have shaped his vision. But I will also try to read his work theologically: to consider it as an attempt to say something truthful about God and human experience. That is, at any rate, how Williams wants to be read. Theology, in his view, is not a private table for one but a rowdy banquet of those who gather, famished and thirsty, around Christ. The lonely work of reading and writing is not yet theology but only its preparation. Theology happens wherever we are drawn together into the congenial and annoying labour of conversing, listening, and disputing – in short, where we are drawn into a collective struggle for truthful speech. The aim of Williams' writing is to provoke us into such a struggle, to remind us that truth is not something

---

[1] Rowan Williams, 'A Person That Nobody Knows: A Paradoxical Tribute to Thomas Merton,' *Cistercian Studies* 13:4 (1978), 401.

possessed by any one of us but a promise and a project for which
we have to take responsibility together.

On these terms, theology is a difficult business, frustratingly
imperfect and incomplete – what Augustine sadly called
'inconsummatus.' But by the same token, it is (or can be) a labour
of joy, buoyed up by the good humour, honesty, and generous
attentiveness of friendship. And although I cannot blame this book
on anybody else, I should like to record my gratitude to those
friends and colleagues who have discussed it with me and helped
me to find my way down some of the more daunting back roads of
Williams' work.

I owe a special debt to Kim Fabricius, minister at Bethel United
Reformed Church in Swansea, who first got me reading Rowan Williams
some years ago and who has generously and critically discussed this
book with me at every stage of its gestation. For criticisms of earlier
drafts, and for lively discussions along the way, I thank Oliver Crisp,
Nate Kerr, Scott Stephens, and Steve Wright. I also recall with gratitude
conversations with Stephen Burns, Sarah Coakley, Bob Covolo,
Aaron Ghiloni, Densil Morgan, Janice Rees, and Matheson Russell.
John Walters, vicar of Pontarddulais in Swansea, kindly corresponded
with me regarding Williams' early reading habits, and Rupert Shortt and
Scott Stephens provided me with a typescript of Williams' unpublished
1974 lectures on T. S. Eliot.

My chronological interpretation of Williams' work could
not have been possible without Rupert Shortt's two biographies,
Rowan Williams: An Introduction (London: Darton, Longman &
Todd, 2003) and *Rowan's Rule: The Biography of the Archbishop*
(London: Hodder & Stoughton, 2008). I have learned a great deal
from Mike Higton's thematic study, *Difficult Gospel: The Theology
of Rowan Williams* (London: SCM, 2004), and I have made constant
use of the extensive bibliography of Williams' work compiled by
Matheson Russell, in *On Rowan Williams: Critical Essays* (Eugene,
OR: Cascade, 2009), as well as Mike Higton's online bibliography,
available at http://goringe.net/theology.

I am also grateful to Rowan Williams for reading a draft of the
manuscript and for answering my queries on various biographical
points.

And last of all (but also first): Elise.

Introduction

The German writer Karl Kraus once observed that the more closely you look at a word, the more distantly it looks back. We have all experienced that uncanny moment when a long-familiar word becomes strange and remote. And the experience is not confined to language. When you consider any object closely enough, the façade of self-evidence starts to peel away, and you catch a glimpse of the unaccountable otherness of what is there – 'the startling wetness of water' or the 'unutterable muddiness of mud,' as G. K. Chesterton memorably put it.[1] Each thing is different, strange, unique; the distance between things becomes visible only when you get close enough – as though difference were something that cannot be glimpsed until it's right under your nose.

That is Rowan Williams' characteristic habit of mind: to look at something so intently that it becomes remote and unfamiliar. Like Chesterton, Williams is one of those people who take 'a fierce pleasure in things being themselves.' But what does it tell us about the world if we discover difference only through close attention? What does it mean for human relationships if our real difference from one another becomes visible only in settings of intimate proximity?

These are the questions Williams has been pursuing throughout four decades of theological thinking. Eventually, such questions drive him into the arms of an even greater riddle: why is it the case that our world is organized like this? Are there clues about the source of life in our fumbling, awkward attempts to get to know one another and to discover ourselves through one another? Does every difference finally point beyond itself to the mystery of an infinitely near-yet-distant God? That is the basic movement of Williams' thought: from the puzzle of human sociality to the mystery of God.

Joan Chittister recently observed that Williams 'deals with scenes from everyday life with the eye of a realist who believes in God.'[2] If

---

[1] Maisie Ward, *Gilbert Keith Chesterton* (New York: Sheed & Ward, 1942), 97.

[2] Joan Chittister and Rowan Williams, *Uncommon Gratitude: Alleluia for All That Is* (Collegeville: Liturgical Press, 2010), xi.

there is something instantly recognizable in Williams' writing, it is this 'eye,' this unsentimental attention to the peculiar texture of everyday experience and to the surprising ways in which such experience points beyond itself to divine mystery. It is what Simone Weil called *attente*: not a passive waiting, but a wide-eyed attention and expectancy. More like birdwatching than watching television; more like waiting for Christmas than waiting for the 9:45 train to Liverpool. That is what gives Williams' writing its peculiar arresting quality, its capacity to induce moments of surprise and wakefulness. His imagination is like that of England's priest–poet, George Herbert: not a grand sweeping vision, but a patient, inquisitive attention to small things, a habit of setting ordinary things in a new light by relating them to God. 'Heaven in ordinary':[3] that is Williams' way of seeing the world.

In an address to the House of Bishops in 2003, Elizabeth Templeton asked the bishops to consider how they would respond to the following scenario. On the street one day, a man walks up and says, 'My bus leaves in two minutes. Tell me about the resurrection in the time remaining.' Templeton supplied her own humorous solution: 'If you really want to hear about the resurrection, be prepared to miss your bus.' But Rowan scratched his beard for a moment, then suggested a different answer: 'I think I'd have asked the man where he was going, then said that I'd accompany him on the journey.'[4] That is a picture of the way Williams does theology: he glimpses the scene from a subtly different perspective; his imagination seizes on a detail that we had somehow failed to notice. And once we have seen the situation in this new light, our capacity to act seems dramatically enlarged.

If I were to give a name to this peculiar habit of seeing, I suppose I would have to call it *poetic*. The poet is someone who looks at language so closely that it becomes new, so that what was always familiar now seems utterly singular and arresting. Our normal perceptions are dim and dreamlike, but the poet rouses us to attention – not really to see something new, but to see anew what was right there in front of us all along. Williams' theological writing is animated by this poetic sensibility. He wants not to tell us something new but to draw our

---

[3] George Herbert, 'Prayer I,' in *The English Poems of George Herbert*, ed. Helen Wilcox (Cambridge: Cambridge University Press, 2007).

[4] The anecdote is related in Rupert Shortt, *Rowan's Rule: The Biography of the Archbishop* (London: Hodder & Stoughton, 2008), 320–21.

attention to things that we have always known yet somehow never really *seen*. That's why he likes to take familiar religious language and to tease out its inherent difficulties, paradoxes, and limitations. Such analysis might seem tortuous at times, but its aim is to capture the sheer oddness of Christian belief, to bring us back into contact with the strangeness of our speech.

A recent incident reported in *The Telegraph* is a typical example.[5] A 6-year-old Scottish girl named Lulu wrote a letter to God: 'To God: How did you get invented?' Lulu's father, who is not a believer, sent her letter to the Archbishop of Canterbury. He promptly sent the following letter in reply:

Dear Lulu,

Your dad has sent on your letter and asked if I have any answers. It's a difficult one! But I think God might reply a bit like this –

'Dear Lulu – Nobody invented me – but lots of people discovered me and were quite surprised. They discovered me when they looked round at the world and thought it was really beautiful or really mysterious and wondered where it came from. They discovered me when they were very very quiet on their own and felt a sort of peace and love they hadn't expected. Then they invented ideas about me – some of them sensible and some of them not very sensible. From time to time I sent them some hints – specially in the life of Jesus – to help them get closer to what I'm really like. But there was nothing and nobody around before me to invent me. Rather like somebody who writes a story in a book, I started making up the story of the world and eventually invented human beings like you who could ask me awkward questions!'

And then he'd send you lots of love and sign off. I know he doesn't usually write letters, so I have to do the best I can on his behalf. Lots of love from me too.

+Archbishop Rowan

It is a touching letter, shot through with that imaginative oddness which is always so recognizable in Williams' writing. And the whole letter reflects one of his deepest religious convictions: that talking about

---

[5] Reported by Damian Thompson in *The Telegraph* 22 April 2011.

God does not require a specialized vocabulary or an esoteric religious experience. Everyday human experience and everyday language can become windows into God's activity. The many different styles and genres of Williams' work all approach their tasks from this same starting point, a trust that God's activity is intimately accessible, available right here in the midst of ordinary embodied life with others.

Yet attention to God is never easy. God may be 'more inward to me than my innermost self,'[6] but it is that very nearness that makes God so strange and different. Think of marriage: there is no one more mysterious than a spouse – not because they are distant and unfamiliar, but because they are so near and so well known. God, too, is near and hard to grasp. This paradox runs right through Williams' work. It is the paradox of the intimate distance between God and human experience: the paradox of incarnation.

Theologians often invoke metaphors of building to describe their work: the scholar as a grand architect, a wise foreman, an honest bricklayer. But for Williams, theology is less like a construction site than like a friendship. Not a monument to be built but something collectively ventured, explored, revised, negotiated, threatened by subtle conflicts and enlarged by subtle graces. It is a sort of intellectual 'zigzag,' to borrow an image from Sergius Bulgakov; a 'shaky, fluctuating path' towards truthful speech.[7] Theology then is not a solitary endeavour; personal relationships of loving opposition are the necessary environment for the zigzag of Christian imagination.

This means that theology is a risky business, and there will be no legitimate way to keep it safe. It is 'dangerous thought,'[8] thought balanced on the edge of a knife. From the 1970s to the present, Williams has given ample testimony to the riskiness of Christian thinking. You can see it in the widespread international alarm provoked by his recent lecture on British jurisprudence and sharia law.[9] You can see it in the way he has raised challenging questions

---

[6] Augustine, *Confessions*, 3.6.11.

[7] Sergius Bulgakov, *The Bride of the Lamb* [1945], trans. Boris Jakim (Grand Rapids: Eerdmans, 2002), 143–44.

[8] Rowan Williams, '"Adult Geometry": Dangerous Thoughts in R. S. Thomas,' in *The Page's Drift: R. S. Thomas at Eighty*, ed. M. Wynn Thomas (Bridgend: Seren Books, 1993).

[9] Rowan Williams, 'Civil and Religious Law in England: A Religious Perspective,' 7 February 2008 <http://www.archbishopofcanterbury.org/1575>.

about human sexuality, trying to rethink Christian identity itself in the context of sexual desire.[10] You can see it in his writing on spirituality, with its sharp accent on God's 'anarchic mercy'[11] and on the psychological fragmentation and ambiguity of human life before God. You can see it in his moral thinking, where even a youth's desperate suicide can be dimly but shockingly perceived as a legitimate protest against the world's intolerable disorder, and so as 'a converted act' which points to the hope of the gospel.[12]

Clearly, Williams doesn't mind taking a few risks. He doesn't expect Christian thinking to be safe or easy. Indeed, he once remarked that the best theology is like 'the noise of someone falling over things in the dark'[13] – an awkward, inelegant testimony to the God who rearranges the furniture of our lives. This is the God who 'enters into a world of confusion and ambiguity, and works in contradictions.'[14] After all, even God's own self-communication in our world was not a unilateral declaration but an appalling, ambiguous zigzag of death and resurrection. Such a God does not console us or fulfil our wishes but strips us of our fantasies and brings our religious expectations under judgement.

In this book, I want to give an account of Williams' theology by describing the conversations and encounters through which his distinctive imaginative vision has emerged over time. Naturally, I cannot hope to explore everything he has written or every debate in which he has participated. Instead, I will try to identify those texts and encounters that have left indelible marks on his thought or have caused his imagination to strike out in a new direction. My aim is not to summarize Williams' views on various topics but to uncover the sources of his ideas, to trace the overall direction

---

[10] Rowan Williams, *The Body's Grace: The 10th Michael Harding Memorial Address* (London: Lesbian and Gay Christian Movement, 1989).

[11] Rowan Williams, *The Wound of Knowledge: Christian Spirituality from the New Testament to St. John of the Cross* [1979] (2nd ed.; London: Darton, Longman & Todd, 1990), 17.

[12] Rowan Williams, *Resurrection: Interpreting the Easter Gospel* [1982] (2nd ed.; Cleveland, OH: Pilgrim Press, 2002), 42.

[13] Rowan Williams, 'Telling the Christmas Story Like It Is,' *The Guardian* 23 December 2000.

[14] Williams, *The Wound of Knowledge*, 14.

of his intellectual development, and to explore the deeper cultural problems to which his work is (often only implicitly) responding.

My interpretation of his work follows a chronological path and may be said to fall into three broad periods:

- *First*, an early period from the 1970s to the late 1980s, dominated by the Wittgensteinian question of the relation between language and sociality.

- *Second*, a middle period from the late 1980s to the late 1990s, dominated by the Hegelian question of whether a social order is more than the sum of its parts.

- *Third*, a later period from the end of the 1990s to the present, dominated by the Freudian question of whether human desire is necessarily trapped in selfish fantasy or whether human beings can enter into that mode of relating which the New Testament calls 'love.'

When Karl Barth sat down to write the *Church Dogmatics*, he started with the doctrine of the trinity and then spent the rest of his life figuring out the implications. Williams begins, rather modestly, with the puzzles of ordinary human relationships. And this sets him on a long, meandering path that leads finally – as though by accident – to the mystery of the trinity. That is the story I hope to tell in this book.

PROLOGUE

Most theology is made of words. But there is also such a thing as visual theology: paintings, sculptures, and icons have their own mute eloquence, their own capacity to bear witness to the curious texture of divine life. Such visual theology recurs like a leitmotif in the poetry of Rowan Williams. His 2008 poem, 'Resurrection: Borgo San Sepolcro,'[1] reflects on Piero della Francesca's fifteenth-century masterpiece, *Resurrection* (Figure 1) – a painting that Aldous Huxley called 'the greatest picture in the world.' Williams writes:

> Today it is time. Warm enough, finally,
> to ease the lids apart, the wax lips of a breaking bud
> defeated by the steady push, hour after hour,
> opening to show wet and dark, a tongue exploring,
> an eye shrinking against the dawn. Light
> like a fishing line draws its catch straight up,
> then slackens for a second. The flat foot drops,
> the shoulders sag. Here is the world again, well-known,
> the dawn greeted in snoring dreams of a familiar
> winter everyone prefers. So the black eyes
> fixed half-open, start to search, ravenous,
> imperative, they look for pits, for hollows where
> their flood can be decanted, look
> for rooms ready for commandeering, ready
> to be defeated by the push, the green implacable
> rising. So he pauses, gathering the strength
> in his flat foot, as the perspective buckles under him,

---

[1] Rowan Williams, 'Resurrection: Borgo San Sepolcro,' in *Headwaters* (Oxford: Perpetua Press, 2008), 26.

FIGURE 1   Piero della Francesca, *Resurrection*, c. 1460. Photo credit: akg-images/
Electa.

and the dreamers lean dangerously inwards. Contained,
exhausted, hungry, death running off his limbs like drops
from a shower, gathering himself. We wait,
paralysed as if in dreams, for his spring.

Christ is rising. Time is pressed tight like a spring. The painting
captures that moment at the dawn of the third day when Christ
emerges from death into life. 'Today it is time': the poem draws
attention to this split second, where all God's work is compressed

into a single point. There is something almost nightmarish in Williams' depiction of Christ majestically stepping out from the grave, 'death running off his limbs like drops/from a shower.' That is the moment captured by Piero's picture: Christ is halfway risen; he has paused to gather himself for a final spring; his shoulders sag indolently, his flat foot resting on the sarcophagus. The 'black eyes' that have seen the depths of hell now stare out, ravenous not with hunger but with an unbearable fullness. His deathless life is wild and uncontainable; like an overflowing cup, he seeks out smaller vessels into which his own life can be decanted. His eyes are commanding, imperative, searching out those whose lives are ready – like the tomb – to be pushed open and 'defeated' by his implacable rising.

In the painting, Piero uses multiple perspectives, so that we are uncertain of our own relationship to the scene. Viewing the picture on the wall in Sansepolcro, we seem to be looking up at the sleeping soldiers; but then Christ shifts the perspective, and we find ourselves situated slightly higher than his foot, as though we were standing above the sleeping figures. And then, looking up, we discover that Christ's eyes are looking not down at us but straight ahead. There are at least three different perspectives here, depending on where we look. So in Williams' poem, Christ's rising seems to alter the very shape of reality, as though geometry itself were bending beneath him, just as the geometry of our lives buckles under the weight of his rising. Hence the sleepers 'lean dangerously inwards,' their forms responding to these distortions in perspective, while we too 'lean inwards' as we feel the ineluctable magnetism of Christ's summons. He is reordering our world, intruding his authority upon us, boring into us with his piercing black eyes. From his flat foot, Christ will momentarily spring like an athlete from the grave; and the resurrection is likewise the end of winter, the 'spring' in which every flower blooms.

In an earlier poem, 'Pantocrator: Daphni' (1994),[2] Williams describes the Pantocrator mosaic in the monastery of Daphni in Greece (Figure 2). The Pantocrator is one of the central images of Orthodox iconography. In its typical form, it portrays Christ as ruler and judge: his authoritative face looks directly at the

---

[2] Rowan Williams, 'Pantocrator: Daphni,' in *The Poems of Rowan Williams* (Grand Rapids: Eerdmans, 2002), 47.

FIGURE 2 Christ Pantocrator mosaic from Daphni, Greece, c. 1080–1100. Photo credit: The Yorck Project, DirectMedia/Wikipedia.

worshipper, while his left hand holds the book of the Gospels and his right is raised in a gesture of blessing or teaching. The eleventh-century mosaic in Daphni, however, departs strikingly from this form. Christ's eyes look not at the worshipper but away to one side, and the perspective of the eyes is strangely distorted. Instead of holding a book with serene authority, the figure clutches it with long, desperate fingers. The right hand is lowered; it imparts no teaching, communicates no blessing. Williams' poem draws attention to these unconventional aspects of the image:

Pillars of dusty air beneath the dome
of golden leaden sky strain to bear up
his sweaty heaviness, his bulging eyes
drawn inwards to their private pain,
his hands arthritic with those inner knots,
his blessings set aside.
He has forgotten us, this once,
and sees a black unvisitable place
where from all ages to all ages he will die
and cry, creating in his blood
congealing galaxies of heat and weight.
Why should he bless or need an open book?
we know the words as well as he,
the names, Alpha, Omega,
fire from fire, we know your cry
out of the dusty golden whirlwind, how you forget
us so that we can be.[3]

In a place of Christian worship, what could be more familiar than
the face of Christ? Yet in this fleeting moment he has looked away,
and we find ourselves gazing up into the face of a stranger. His
thoughts are sealed up in a place beyond our reach. There is a
sort of remote intimacy about this moment, as Christ neglects to
hold the official pose of a benevolent Pantocrator. In a moment
of forgetfulness, he glances into that 'black unvisitable place,' the
abyssal horror of Gethsemane and Golgotha. We have intruded on
this most private of moments; we are eavesdroppers on a pain that
is older than the world. Through eternal ages Christ will always
remember us, only because this once he forgets: 'you forget/us so
that we can be.'

Creation buckles under the weight of this agony, the 'sweaty
heaviness' of all his sorrow. In the intensity of Christ's inner
turmoil, he can no longer hold the gesture of blessing; his hands
clutch arthritically with the pain of those 'inner knots,' and, just
for a second, all blessings are set aside. Looking into the darkness
of Golgotha, he lurches back into the brooding depths of creation,
where the swirling galaxies take form in his own congealing blood.

---

[3] The text in *The Poems of Rowan Williams* mistakenly has 'one' instead of 'once' in
line 7.

His wounds cut deep into the sinews of eternity; he has bled forever, crying while his blood brought forth the 'heat and weight' of all the worlds. 'There was a cross in the heart of God before there was one planted on the green hill outside Jerusalem.'[4] The crucifixion is Christ's whole identity, his alpha and omega: he is *named* for this.

In the poem's final image, this suffering Christ is identified as the same one whom Job met – the one who clothed himself in the terrors of the storm and proclaimed the mighty deeds of creation: 'Then the Lord answered Job out of the whirlwind . . . . Where wast thou when I laid the foundations of the earth?' (Job 38.1–4). Here, though, it is the tortured cry of the crucified Christ that thunders from the whirlwind. Now God speaks not with majestic omnipotence but with a desolate sob. The whole great drama of the creation and redemption of the world is compressed into that one appalling sound: the cry of a broken Pantocrator, the inarticulate utterance of the Word.

---

[4] C. A. Dinsmore, *Atonement in Literature and Life* (Boston: Houghton & Mifflin, 1906), 232.

1

Sociality

How do we avoid
A treaty with the compromising word?[1]

One afternoon in the middle of the 1960s, a scruffy Welsh teenager
sat cross-legged on the ground upon a windswept headland, intently
reading a dog-eared paperback while the crying gulls wheeled above
him and the grey sea foamed against the rocks along the shore. He
finished the last page – it was something by Wittgenstein – and looked
for a long time across the bay, while the book lay open in his lap and
his bare toes twitched in the grass. Then he got up, shoved the book
in his coat pocket, and made his way slowly back up the hill towards
the house, limping slightly as he went. Rain clouds had darkened the
sky; tonight it would be cold, even indoors.

Rowan Williams grew up here, in Swansea, a coastal town in
the south of Wales – a group of villages held together by gossip, as
a local saying has it. One former resident, the poet Dylan Thomas,
called it an 'ugly, lovely town.' That may be true enough: the town's
inauspicious brick houses squat in the shadow of the old copper
works, the little suburbs huddle modestly in their white caps along
the hills, a towering viaduct rises up above the poisoned river. But
it is also a place of wild anarchic beauty: the town looks out across
the brooding darkness of the sea, while the vast open moors stretch
away to the north. Swansea is known for its strong university
and rich intellectual heritage, and the young Rowan Williams, an
uncommonly quiet and bookish boy, was shaped by that heritage.
As an infant, he had been very ill with meningitis, and he was never
able to play sports or ride a bicycle or generally run about as most

---

[1] Rowan Williams, 'Crossings,' in *The Poems of Rowan Williams* (Grand Rapids:
Eerdmans, 2002), 33.

boys do. So from an early age he withdrew into the slower, solitary consolations of literature, philosophy, and history: already by the age of 13, people would remark on his wide reading.

His discovery of the philosophy of Wittgenstein at a young age was more than accidental. The Austrian philosopher had an intimate connection to Swansea. His close friend Rush Rhees was a professor at Swansea University, and Wittgenstein had spent his summer holidays in the town throughout the 1940s. Rhees, who later became the executor of Wittgenstein's literary estate, was the first to develop a religious interpretation of Wittgenstein's work, and since the 1950s this approach had dominated Swansea's philosophy department. So the troubled figure of Wittgenstein was part of the history and culture of the town. Indeed, Williams first heard about Wittgenstein from one of his neighbours who taught history at the university; so it is eccentric, but not inexplicable, to find our barefoot schoolboy sitting alone on a Swansea headland pondering the hard sayings of Wittgenstein on one of those grey autumn afternoons of the 1960s.

The later Wittgenstein had criticized the view that individual words have meanings or that meaning resides in any describable logical system. Meaning, he said, is produced only in specific contexts of social interaction. You can understand meaning only when you look at 'the practice of language.'[2] Language is something we *do*, and confusion arises whenever this is forgotten. For example, philosophers exhaust themselves in arguments over the nature of the good, whereas there is no such thing as 'the good,' only various human acts which are called 'good' through a sort of family resemblance.[3] This means we cannot view language as a self-contained system – a sort of dictionary, crammed full of discrete parcels of meaning – but we have to observe the whole form of life within which a language operates. There is no such thing as a 'private language,' since language could have no meaning outside a shared form of life.

If Wittgenstein was not exactly outspoken about religion or theology, Rush Rhees and his colleagues at Swansea University – known among Wittgenstein scholars as the Swansea school – were

---

[2] Ludwig Wittgenstein, *On Certainty* (Oxford: Blackwell, 1975), §501.

[3] Ludwig Wittgenstein, *Philosophical Grammar*, ed. Rush Rhees (Oxford: Blackwell, 1974), 77.

busily teasing out the religious implications of this philosophy. The Swansea school was marked not only by a religious emphasis but also by an interest in literature, to a degree quite unheard of in other philosophy departments at the time. In Swansea, philosophers tested and developed their thinking through engagements with writers of fiction like Tolstoy, Dostoevsky, Melville, Conrad, Hemingway, and Flannery O'Connor; and with poets like T. S. Eliot and R. S. Thomas. They saw literature not merely as a device to illustrate more general philosophical truths but as a vital intellectual resource in its own right, a way of uncovering the truth and particularity of human experience.[4] Literature, with its attention to the particular, was an antidote to philosophical confusion.

Wittgenstein had condemned the 'craving for generality' in philosophy.[5] For the Swansea school, a commitment to particulars – particular forms of life, particular experiences, particular practices – meant that all tendencies towards generality had to be stringently resisted. Theology is not a system of ideas. It is part of a wider religious language that operates within embodied patterns of ritual life and religious observance. As one of Williams' later teachers, the Wittgensteinian theologian Fergus Kerr, observed: 'If we cannot imagine what it is to observe rites, enjoy singing hymns and the like, the nature of religion is bound to remain opaque.'[6] The priority of life over ideas: that is what gripped Williams' imagination as a young Welsh reader of Wittgenstein.

This habit of mind has left a lasting impression on Williams' thought; decades later, it continues to orient his thinking about Christ, the church, and society. That is one of the reasons for the distinctiveness of his writing. Whether he is writing about a fourth-century theological debate, a sixteenth-century mystic, or a nineteenth-century novelist, there is something immediately recognisable in the *way* he reads texts, and in the kinds of questions he poses to the past. He reads like a Swansea Wittgensteinian, asking not simply about ideas, but how those ideas are used, how they operate within wider social environments. He interprets

---

[4] Mario von der Ruhr, 'Rhees, Wittgenstein, and the Swansea School,' in *Sense and Reality: Essays out of Swansea*, ed. John Edelman (Heusenstamm: Ontos Verlag, 2009).

[5] Ludwig Wittgenstein, *The Blue and Brown Books* (Oxford: Blackwell, 1958), 17.

[6] Fergus Kerr, *Theology after Wittgenstein* (Oxford: Blackwell, 1986), 183.

language according to its use in specific communities; he reads texts as reflections on life; he judges Christian ideas not only by their internal coherence, but by their coherence with Christian practice. From Wittgenstein he learned to ask not about words but about meanings, not about individuals but about social life, not about the general but about particulars, and not just about what people believe but about the way they behave. Above all, Williams' early reading of Wittgenstein prompted him to think about human sociality itself as a theological reality, and that is what drew him, some years later, to the tradition of Russian Orthodoxy.

When Williams went to Oxford for doctoral studies, instead of selecting a small, carefully circumscribed topic for his research, he did just the opposite. He chose to study an entire *world*: the darkly luxuriant world of Russian Orthodoxy. In a period of intensive study, he worked his way through some of the major figures of modern Russian thought – Pavel Florensky, Sergius Bulgakov, Paul Evdokimov, as well as the Greek Orthodox philosopher Christos Yannaras – before finally settling on the Russian émigré theologian Vladimir Lossky. It would be impossible to exaggerate the importance of Russian thought in the shaping of Williams' imagination. Since the 1970s, even his physical appearance has been stylized after the customs of Russian piety – not least in his obvious sympathy with 'the unanimous struggle of Russians against the shaving of beards.'[7] Even today, the Archbishop of Canterbury is best understood not as an Anglican with an interest in Orthodoxy but as essentially 'Orthodox in an Anglican form.'[8]

In his doctoral thesis, completed in 1975, Williams explores Lossky's understanding of 'negative' or 'apophatic' theology, where we speak of God by saying what God is *not*. Unlike most of his contemporaries in Oxford, he was concerned here not with familiar questions about the nature of religious language but with the relation of theology and spirituality, divine life and social life, human

---

[7] Pavel Florensky, *The Pillar and Ground of the Truth* [1914], trans. Boris Jakim (Princeton: Princeton University Press, 1997), 217. Florensky refers to seventeenth-century Russians who protested against Peter the Great's imposed beard-shaving: 'let them rather chop off our heads than shave our beards!'

[8] Rupert Shortt, *Rowan's Rule: The Biography of the Archbishop* (London: Hodder & Stoughton, 2008), 79. The phrase was used of Williams' doctoral supervisor, Donald Allchin.

persons and the persons of the trinity. Negative theology, he argues, can never be 'a move in a conceptual game'; it is not a technique, or a linguistic trick, or a clever way of circumventing obstacles in our language about God. It is rather a process of transformation, a conversion of the intellect – or rather, a conversion of the whole self – whereby we are drawn outside ourselves into the presence of someone who is different.[9] According to Lossky, the doctrine of the trinity is a crucifixion of the intellect, 'a cross for human ways of thought.'[10] If the cross is a revelation of God's identity, then personality itself – what it means to be a person – is revealed as a 'kenotic' reality. In the trinity, there is no self-interest, no 'individual will,' but only an enormous movement of painful, ecstatic self-renunciation. This self-renouncing pattern of life is the root of all personal being.[11]

The self-directed autonomous individual, therefore, is a picture not of what it means to be human but of what it means to be fallen: think of Milton's Satan. The image of God lies not somewhere 'inside' the self but 'outside.' We begin to reflect God, and to become truly human, only as we pull away from our own interests and attach ourselves to the interests of others. Indeed for Lossky, the autonomous self is a sort of blasphemy, a broken mirror that reflects God's image as a grotesque and diabolical disfigurement. Only in the social exchange of kenotic selves, each going beyond itself towards another, is God's image restored. Humanness is not wholeness, self-mastery, self-containment: we are most human when we are cracked, when each self bleeds out into the lives of others.

This doctrine of the human person poses sharp challenges to the western assumption that the self is a determinate 'essence,' more or less transparent to rational analysis. What can it mean to know someone, if what really constitutes a person is not positive qualities like freedom or rationality but something negative: kenosis, self-renunciation, the crucifixion of the self? Human persons can be

---

[9] Rowan Williams, 'Lossky, the *Via Negativa* and the Foundations of Theology' [1979], in *Wrestling with Angels*, ed. Mike Higton (Grand Rapids: Eerdmans, 2007), 2. This published essay was adapted from Williams' 1975 doctoral thesis, 'The Theology of Vladimir Nikolaevich Lossky: An Exposition and Critique.'

[10] Vladimir Lossky, *The Mystical Theology of the Eastern Church* (Cambridge: James Clarke, 1957), 66.

[11] Williams, 'Lossky,' 14–15.

known only negatively or apophatically, since personhood is itself a sort of negative property. We can never define what it is to be a person, since the 'personal' element is exactly what remains most dark and unknowable in another. Human persons then are the image of God to the extent that they reflect God's unknowability, the mystery of crucified selfhood. Lossky can even say that each human person is 'as mysterious and unimaginable' as the trinity itself.[12] Mystery is not the opposite of knowing; it is the exact content of what we know about others.

Williams brings his Wittgensteinian imagination to bear on this Russian theology of personhood. The difficulty of all social exchange lies in the fact that human persons must always remain strange and mysterious to one another. You can never achieve a complete understanding of another person; the better you know someone, the more mysterious they become. Social life, therefore, is not about collapsing differences or engineering an artificial unity. Instead differences should be accentuated as sharply as possible, so that what you experience in another person is not fantasy, not another deceptive projection of yourself, but the real intractable mystery of another self. You can never be done with another person, since every advance in knowing is an opening on to greater mystery. In every social exchange, we are moving about the edges of a deep well: the closer you come to another human self, the further down you can see. It is in the most intimate proximity to others that we are most painfully aware of their difference: that is, for instance, what makes marriage the most demanding, and often the most tragic, form of human relating.

Understanding another person, then, is never a completed task but only a continuing labour. Here, every success is an even greater failure, every beam of light a ray of darkness. As Williams has observed more recently in a comment on the plays of Shakespeare, there is 'a huge hinterland, a huge ... darkness behind the eyes and the faces of people, which we never encompass, we never get around.'[13]

This sense of the intractable strangeness of other selves is one of Williams' deepest and most enduring intuitions. He is often

---

[12] Lossky, *Mystical Theology*, 92, 118.

[13] BBC interview with Jim Naughtie, 24 April 2006, 'Shakespeare: The Today Programme': http://www.archbishopofcanterbury.org/articles.php/755/shakespeare-the-today-programme.

described as an advocate of negative theology, though his work in these early years was always more concerned with what it means to be a human person and with how a meaningful encounter between persons becomes possible. These questions emerged as much from Wittgenstein as from Russian Orthodoxy. Indeed, all Williams' early work on Russian theology is haunted by a larger Wittgensteinian question: how can meaning be shared across two different Christian traditions, those vastly disparate forms of life represented by the Latin west and the Orthodox east?

In one of his earliest published essays, a study of the philosophy of Christos Yannaras, Williams cautions that western writers are often 'hypnotized by sheer novelty' when they first encounter eastern traditions.[14] If Williams himself was never quite hypnotized – in the 1970s he briefly flirted with the notion of leaving the Church of England for Orthodoxy, but soon dismissed the idea – it is perhaps because he is so intrigued by the site of encounter between differences, the points at which western and eastern traditions might productively collide. A conversion to Orthodoxy would have betrayed his love of difference.

That is why his work on Orthodoxy remains unhampered by that nostalgic romanticizing tendency that sheds a soft light on so much western writing about the east. Williams feels sharply the tensions between these different traditions, but he wants to sustain the tensions in his own thought, to resist the easy catharsis of a capitulation from one side to the other. How can we share and exchange meaning while allowing another tradition to be as strange and as particular as it really is? That is the question that drives his restless expeditions into the imagination of the Christian east.

Throughout his career, Williams has continued to probe those sensitive boundaries, those jagged edges along which different selves and different traditions meet. What happens when differences collide? How can these collisions be negotiated? How can they change us and enlarge us? How can they draw us out beyond ourselves instead of making us retreat into the safety of our own private worlds? How can we really *see* one another truthfully without merely projecting our own expectations on to one another?

---

[14] Rowan Williams, 'The Theology of Personhood: A Study of the Thought of Christos Yannaras,' *Sobornost* 6 (1972), 416.

Williams' early encounter with Wittgenstein gave shape to a commitment that has remained foundational to his theological vision: a commitment not to faith as an abstract system of ideas but to Christian sociality as a real, embodied pattern of life. A certain German theologian once quipped that he does not go to church on Sunday mornings; he lies in his hammock and ponders ecclesiology. Is this not the gravest temptation for so many theologians – to imagine the church as a spiritual ideal, a sort of Platonic form of ecclesiality, instead of the disappointingly earthy experience of embodied human community? To stay in your hammock thinking about ecclesiology: that is a recipe not for ecclesiology but for angelology. Rowan Williams thinks that Christ came to create a community not of angels but of real human beings. That is where his view of the church differs from so many others: there are no wings in Williams' theology.

2

Tragedy

Earth is a hard text to read.[1]

I doubt that any of Shakespeare's plays was ever more perfectly realized than Grigori Kozintsev's 1971 film, *King Lear*. It is a fiercely Russian production, set against the gigantic stark landscapes of Soviet Russia and steeped in the dark relentless realism of Gogol and Dostoevsky. The madness of Lear's inner world unfolds amid a wider tragedy that seems to encompass the whole kingdom. As the film opens, a procession of beggars makes its way across a desolate landscape; by the end, as the country is ravaged by the madness of war, Lear has become part of that anonymous procession, one of the 'poor naked wretches' of the earth. In Kozintsev's hands, the play is not so much about singular acts of violence or the enormity of individual suffering as it is about the colossal scale of human tragedy, the way an entire social order can be engulfed by chaos and despair. Yet as the bodies of Lear and Cordelia are carried away at the end, the camera pans across the faces of the survivors – the poor, the ruined, the refugees – and we realize that they will somehow go on living in this 'gored state,' this blighted and disordered world. Here, one of the deep themes of Shakespeare's text comes to the fore: the imperative of patience, of sheer human endurance in the face of meaningless catastrophe. Patience beyond hope: that is the moral vision of tragedy, and it is a vision that has gripped the theological imagination of Rowan Williams. As a youth, he was deeply moved by *King Lear*, the 'uncompromising quality' of its tragic vision and 'the constant refusal to believe in easy answers.'[2]

---

[1] Rowan Williams, 'Die Bibelforscher,' translated from the Welsh of Waldo Williams, in *The Poems of Rowan Williams* (Grand Rapids: Eerdmans, 2002), 106.

[2] Todd Breyfogle, 'Time and Transformation: A Conversation with Rowan Williams,' *Cross Currents* 45:3 (1995).

Before beginning doctoral studies at Oxford, Williams was a young theology student at Cambridge. He had planned on taking a degree in English literature, but at the last minute switched to theology – not as an alternative to literature but as a way of exploring the deeper questions that he had stumbled upon in his reading of authors like Shakespeare, T. S. Eliot, and W. H. Auden. As an adolescent, he had been bored by religious studies; it was poetry that first sparked his interest in theological questions and eventually led him into formal theological study.

The 1960s was a heady time to be reading theology. In Britain, Bishop John A. T. Robinson had achieved celebrity status for the blithe existentialism of *Honest to God*. In North America, leftwing Barthians had gleefully proclaimed the death of God. In New Testament departments, Rudolf Bultmann's disciples were dutifully peeling away layer after layer of the mythology of Christian belief, while, down the corridors, beleaguered professors of divinity retreated into the recondite certainties of Anglo-American analytic philosophy.

But none of these paths held any imaginative appeal for the young Rowan Williams, who had already read more widely than many of his teachers by the time he arrived at Cambridge. Only one of his teachers really grabbed his attention: he soon fell under the spell of the tortured genius of Donald MacKinnon. MacKinnon's philosophical theology was a peculiar blend of a Barthian commitment to the uniqueness of Christ and a metaphysical realism that emphasized the moral priority of tragedy. For MacKinnon, tragic experience functions as a sort of metaphysical proof, a solution to the Kantian problem of the limits of knowledge. When we become aware of 'the extremity of human life,' we are forced to acknowledge the inadequacy of any naturalistic explanation. A figure like Hamlet, or the figure of a saint, is either completely trivial or else it is shot through with transcendent meaning. 'The life of a Socrates or a saint . . . may be regarded as an intimation of the way in which things are.'[3] Tragedy is morally and metaphysically irreducible.

In the same way, MacKinnon refused to think of the problem of evil as an abstract intellectual puzzle. Instead, he returned repeatedly to the figure of Judas Iscariot, as a sort of anti-saint – a paradigmatic

---

[3] Donald MacKinnon, *The Problem of Metaphysics* (Cambridge: Cambridge University Press, 1974), 78, 145.

revelation of the nature of moral evil. For Christians, 'the problem of the evil will *is* the problem of Judas Iscariot.'[4] The gospel of Christ reveals God's grace and healing for all humanity; but the path to this expansive salvation leads through the small gate of Judas Iscariot. At the heart of Christ's story is this tragic subplot of rejection and betrayal. 'The Son of Man goeth as it is written of him: but woe unto that man by whom the Son of Man is betrayed! It had been good for that man if he had not been born' (Mt. 26.24). MacKinnon's thought is haunted by that hard saying from the Gospel of Matthew. What happens to Jesus is a revelation of God: but Judas Iscariot is part of what happens to Jesus, part of the content of God's revelation. There is a surd element in the gospel story, an unaccountable element of waste, as though God could not step through the doorway of our world without casting a shadow.

MacKinnon's tragic vision also underpins his acerbic criticism of the corrupting power of ecclesiastical institutions. The church tends to arrogate to itself the role of a dispenser of salvation; ecclesiastical ritual exercises this power by providing cheap spiritual consolation to the faithful. But Christian worship ought rather expose us to the particularity of Christ: his strangeness, offensiveness, and difficulty. The gospel is more like the harrowing realism of *King Lear* – a drama that yields up a truth only by staring unflinching into the abyss – than the inoffensive optimism of professional religiosity. It is the realism of 'tragedy charged with life like gunpowder.'[5] The moral seriousness of the gospel is the seriousness of tragedy.

At Cambridge in the 1960s, most students were alienated or merely perplexed by MacKinnon's bleak vision and troubled personality (a personality notoriously celebrated in several of Iris Murdoch's novels, as well as in a play by Tom Stoppard). But Williams found his teacher's approach absorbing and compelling, since this tragic interpretation of the gospel resonated with much that Williams had already intuited from his reading in English literature. Indeed the depth of MacKinnon's influence is most clearly gauged by the way Williams was thinking about poetry during his student years. After he had left Cambridge and begun doctoral studies at Oxford, he soon gained a reputation

---

[4] Donald MacKinnon, 'Philosophy and Christology,' in *Borderlands of Theology and Other Essays* (Philadelphia: J. B. Lippincott, 1968), 67.

[5] Grigori Kozintsev, *King Lear: The Space of Tragedy* (Berkeley: University of California Press, 1977), 90.

as an incisive young interpreter of Russian Orthodoxy. When the General Theological Seminary in New York City invited him to deliver a series of public lectures, the 23-year-old scholar chose as his theme the religious vision of T. S. Eliot's *Four Quartets*.

The lectures, delivered in Manhattan in 1974, offer a lucid, arresting, deeply unsettling examination of the relation between tragedy, hope, and redemption.[6] Williams argues that the *Four Quartets* portray the appearance of meaning within an inherently meaningless world. The whole sequence of history is 'empty and trivial' in itself, yet, paradoxically, one event within that sequence – the incarnation – becomes a vehicle of divine meaning. The incarnation is fraught with ambiguity. It is not a 'triumphant epiphany,' but the shipwreck of one particular human life, a life in which God willingly endures the emptiness of history. Faith, then, is never a means of escaping the torment of a bleak world; rather faith endures that torment, finding within the world an ambiguous disclosure of meaning. Thus faith is 'condemned to contradiction.' In this world, Williams argues, there can be no immediate or unquestionable experience of redemption. God's act in the world is concealed in the darkest moment of history, the crucifixion. It is in spite of appearances, Eliot writes, that 'we call this Friday good.' Faith does not escape the perplexity of history, but endures it. 'The demon of doubt . . . is inseparable from the spirit of belief.'[7] As Balachandra Rajan notes in an important early study of the *Four Quartets*, it is the crucible of despair that yields this sudden illumination of truth and meaning. The pattern, Rajan observes, 'is not one of development,' but of 'an understanding, a total tolerance, in which evil and perversity are endured for the sake of the insight they ultimately generate.' A clear-eyed acceptance of the brutal meaninglessness of history is therefore not a renunciation of the world but an act of 'relentless fidelity' to the world as it really is.[8] God's loving endurance of the world produces a new and redemptive vision of what is, in itself, tragically disordered.

---

[6] My quotations of the lectures are from an unpublished typescript.

[7] T. S. Eliot, 'The *Pensées* of Pascal,' in *Selected Essays* (London: Faber & Faber, 1969), 411.

[8] Balachandra Rajan, 'The Unity of the Quartets,' in *T. S. Eliot: A Study of His Writings by Several Hands*, ed. Balachandra Rajan (London: Dennis Dobson, 1947), 86, 95.

Williams concludes the lectures by suggesting that Eliot reminds us 'of the sheer oddity' of Christian belief. God's redemptive work remains hidden, since God redeems the world through the contradiction of the cross. Indeed even in the resurrection, Christ remains 'hidden,' 'inaccessible,' and 'ambiguous.' God is available only in this contradiction, in the negative experience of darkness and dereliction. Nevertheless, for Eliot, any ultimate pessimism must be resisted. Even if faith is always tragic, faith confesses that 'all shall be well.' Williams concludes then that the poem recalls us to 'the real difficulties of theology which are, at root, not intellectual, but personal and imaginative.'

Some years later, in a homily on T. S. Eliot preached in 1984,[9] Williams would again call up the stark theological vision of the *Four Quartets*. The capacity for love, he says, emerges only as we refuse consoling religious fantasy and accept the truth that ours is 'a world of meaninglessness, of destruction, violence, death, and loss.' The impulse to protect ourselves from this hard truth, to project our own reassuring patterns on to the world – this arises from a beguiling illusion, a refusal to see the world as it is. Love emerges only as we are dispossessed of such fantasy. By looking straight into the abyss of the world's 'empty destitution,' our illusions are burned away. Only now, on the other side of self-centred fantasy, can we make room for the work of love and communion. In short, what Williams finds in Eliot's bleakly redemptive vision is the logic of the gospel: death and resurrection, 'unbearable violence' and 'unbearable compassion.' Worldly optimism is a prophylactic against reality. It must be plunged into the purgative crucible – 'redeemed from fire by fire,' as Eliot says. The possibility of the world's transformation then emerges from endurance, from a truthful and unprotected *seeing* of what is really there.

It would be hard to overestimate the importance of Eliot in Williams' thought. Some of his deepest theological convictions are rooted in the dark soil of Eliot's poetry, and throughout his career he has quoted the *Four Quartets* more frequently than any other work. Indeed, his theology never really moves beyond Eliot but only digs more deeply into that fertile imaginative world of the *Quartets* – a world of tragedy, renunciation, and fragile hope.

---

[9] Rowan Williams, 'Lazarus: In Memory of T. S. Eliot,' in *A Ray of Darkness: Sermons and Reflections* (Cambridge, MA: Cowley, 1994).

Throughout this period, Williams himself had also continued to write poetry. Soon after his New York lectures on Eliot, he published one of his first essays, a precociously ambitious manifesto on 'Poetic and Religious Imagination.'[10] The poet, he writes, is a person silenced by a dislocating experience of the world's impenetrability, its 'utter alienness and inaccessibility' to language. Poetry begins with disillusionment: an experience of the limits of language, its failure to be transparent to reality. But disillusionment is not the end. Instead, Williams argues, the poet confronts the failure of language with complete honesty, and then endures this failure in order to go on speaking: 'The return to language requires an act of faith, and an acceptance of the probability of failure.' Such a return to language is grounded in a Wittgensteinian awareness that there are no private or individual meanings, only the shared meanings that we exchange with one another. Part of the vocation of poets is to share with others their experience of the difficulty of language, their hurtful awareness of limitation, frustration, and inarticulacy. It is not the successes of poets but their failures that matter most: poets expand our human capacities by exposing us to the sheer objectivity of language, the way it enables human community while resisting human mastery and control.

Here, Williams returns to the theme of his lectures on Eliot. In the *Four Quartets*, Eliot inserts a comment about his own poetic language: 'That was a way of putting it – not very satisfactory.' A disquieting sentiment: Williams calls it 'one of the most morally and aesthetically shocking lines' of modern literature. The poet ventures to speak not because speech is adequate but because it is a necessary moment in the continuing struggle for meaning. You stake a position not because it is right, but because staking a position is the only way to enter into the process of learning and growth. And this process, Williams says, is 'obscurely redemptive,' since our failure and defeat drive us into a stance of deeper commitment to the world.

What Williams has learned from Eliot, and from MacKinnon, is this tragic moral vision. It is a sort of ethical version of negative theology. Every human act is a small window that opens on to a dark vista. Moral agency becomes possible when we realize the tragic limitation of our action and yet resolve to act anyway. This

---

[10] Rowan Williams, 'Poetic and Religious Imagination,' *Theology* 80 (1977), 178–87. The quotations that follow are from this essay.

is the extreme opposite of natural law ethics, where moral norms
are thought to be embedded objectively in the world. For Williams,
we are to act against the grain of the world, even against the grain
of what is humanly possible. Moral reasoning does not show us the
right way to act; it only exposes the claustrophobic limits of our
capacities. There is no unambiguously good act, no act that escapes
the web of tragic relations in which our lives are enmeshed. Where
moral reasoning tries to evade the tragic dimension, where it posits
any unambiguous good, it becomes an exercise in fantasy and a
failure to accept that God's grace is at work in the real, damaged
world of human experience.

In Gethsemane, Christ prostrates himself on the earth, begging
that the cup might pass from him – and then adds, 'nevertheless
not my will, but thine be done' (Lk. 22.42). That 'nevertheless' is
the salvation of the world. The whole nightmare of world history
is borne up and redeemed by that moment of shattering resolve.
And so we align ourselves with Christ's work only when our own
disappointment with the world resolves itself into an even deeper
commitment, a sort of hope beyond hope, a commitment beyond
despair.

The pattern of such austere ethical commitment is evident in
Eliot's *Little Gidding*, where the endurance of disillusionment
yields finally to a promised (but still hidden) assurance of grace.
The tension between hope and disillusionment, Williams writes, is
'the cost of honesty, of seeing clearly.' This is a tragic stance – but
not a pointless one, since recommitment to the world is the position
from which redemption becomes possible. The world is not just
accepted but 'accepted and transformed.'[11]

God's grace is, after all, most powerfully at work where God is
most hidden: in the lonely shadows of Gethsemane and Golgotha.
It is when the world rejects God that God is most committed to
the world. In the same way, the young Rowan Williams argues
that ethics involves a pattern of endurance, disappointment, and
recommitment. I stake myself; I suffer failure or rejection; I stake
myself again for the sake of a world that has let me down. In such
costly recommitment, human action is aligned, bruised and limping,
with the redemptive activity of the incarnate God.

---

[11] Williams, 'Poetic and Religious Imagination,' 186.

3

Language

Who is it weeps with you to soak
your dust to speaking clay?[1]

In Dorothy Sayers' cycle of radio plays, *The Man Born to Be King*, the Virgin Mary says of the Passion of her son: 'This is reality. From the beginning of time until now, this is the only thing that has ever really happened.'[2] All Williams' early work hangs together as an attempt to show that what happens to Jesus really *matters* – that his death and resurrection are the heart of reality, 'the only thing that ever really happened.' Throughout the 1970s, Williams' attention was fixed single-mindedly on a theology of the cross. In the early 1980s, as a young curate in Cambridge, he turned his attention to the meaning of the resurrection.

In 1981, Williams was invited to give a series of Lent addresses to clergy in the East End of London. The lectures, published the following year as *Resurrection: Interpreting the Easter Gospel*, formed an extended meditation on the New Testament accounts of the resurrection. As in the previous decade, Williams' thinking here remains oriented around questions of language, moral life, and social belonging. Indeed, the book's main argument is that the New Testament's resurrection narratives are about the creation of a new form of life, a new shared language for God. They are 'texts about religious language itself.'[3] Our real problem, Williams thinks,

---

[1] Rowan Williams, 'Augustine,' in *The Poems of Rowan Williams* (Grand Rapids: Eerdmans, 2002), 49.

[2] Dorothy L. Sayers, *The Man Born to Be King* [1943] (San Francisco: Ignatius Press, 1990), 290.

[3] Rowan Williams, *Resurrection: Interpreting the Easter Gospel* [1982] (2nd ed.; Cleveland, OH: Pilgrim Press, 2002), 66–67.

is not that God is too distant but that, in Christ, God has come unbearably near. There is no safe vantage point from which we can speak about God. 'Christians must learn to speak of a God from whom their lives are not to be separated, a God, therefore, involved with the whole fabric of their being.'[4]

This approach again owes much to the work of Williams' former teacher, Donald MacKinnon. In a 1966 dialogue with G. W. H. Lampe, MacKinnon had criticized both liberal and conservative readings of the resurrection. For the former, the resurrection is myth, while for the latter it is a verifiable historical event: but these are just two sides of the same coin. Whether they affirm the event or deny it, both are 'at home with it'; it is simply 'an event which did or did not happen.'[5] MacKinnon urges instead that the resurrection transcends what we normally understand as history. It lies deep down at the roots of things. It is 'more than event,' more than anything that could merely be proven or observed.

MacKinnon provides no easy answers about the meaning of the resurrection. He is more concerned to render the difficulty of this event, to demonstrate the ways in which it eludes our grasp and overwhelms all our attempts to describe it. In a statement that could easily serve as a summary of Williams' theological style, MacKinnon observes:

> I sometimes think that only when we bring out into the open what it is that defeats our every attempt to handle the things of the Christian faith confidently and without hesitation, will we be able to perceive at least a small measure of its uniqueness.[6]

For Williams as for MacKinnon, theology is not meant to clear things up but to perform a kind of semantic unravelling. The resurrection is not what we thought: it is more, it is different, it is every bit as strange and unique as the creation of the world from nothing. As that which generates our language about God, the resurrection stands beyond the reach of language. It is (to borrow an image from G. K. Chesterton) like the sun: we can't see it directly, but by its light we see everything else.

---

[4] Williams, *Resurrection*, 87.

[5] Donald MacKinnon and G. W. H. Lampe, *The Resurrection: A Dialogue Arising from Broadcasts* (London: Mowbray, 1966), 63.

[6] MacKinnon, *The Resurrection*, 85.

Williams argues that the Christian tradition began with an event of rupture, a traumatic disturbance of existing meanings and forms of social belonging. The resurrection of Jesus from the dead is 'an event on the frontier of any possible language,' since it shatters our speech and our ways of making sense of the world.[7] The founding Christian narratives are likewise subversive and disruptive. The different Easter stories, so confusing, disorienting, and at times contradictory, testify to the sheer impossibility of articulating the Easter event itself. Something has happened here that cannot be integrated into our experience; we have no adequate way to describe it or to capture its meaning. The Christian tradition is generated by this bewildering event and by the alarming narratives that speak of it. Thus, the social patterns of early Christianity are marked by a profound sense of rupture and discontinuity. Right from the start, the church is aware that its own social life is the result of a violent rending of existing systems of meaning. Christian language takes shape as part of a whole new form of human community. When Williams wrestles with the ambiguities of the New Testament accounts, then, he is not trying to explain Christ's resurrection, but to evoke something of this startling uniqueness, the rupture marked out by the early Christian confession that Christ is risen.

Though he never makes it explicit, Williams' underlying metaphor here is that of psychological trauma. In Freudian terms, trauma occurs where the protective shield around the ego is shattered by a powerful external force. This has a permanent effect on the whole functioning of the self: the trauma makes us who we are. Williams had been studying Freud around this time,[8] and though he never mentions Freud in the resurrection book, his account is oriented around a Freudian concept of trauma. The Christian tradition is like the adult self: often outwardly stable, but inwardly shocked and shaken by an inaccessible originating wound. Christ's resurrection is the root – and also the permanent disturbance – of Christian identity. This complex psychoanalytic metaphor gives Williams a way of linking past and present, of articulating the mysterious connection between the church as a form of life extended through time and Christ's

---

[7] Williams, *Resurrection*, 89.

[8] Rowan Williams, 'Freudian Psychology,' in *The Westminster Dictionary of Christian Theology*, ed. Alan Richardson and John Bowden (Philadelphia: Westminster, 1983).

resurrection as a real event of the past which nevertheless remains central to Christian language and experience in the present.

Around the same time, Williams developed this theme in one of his most starkly paradoxical sermons, 'A Ray of Darkness.'[9] Here he depicts Jesus as God's attack on language. Jesus is God's *logos*, the fullness of divine meaning enfleshed in one vulnerable human life. This divine *logos* enters into the structures of human language, but language buckles under its weight. We cannot sustain all that Jesus means; the coming of Christ is the dissolution of speech, since God's *logos* is an alien utterance that cannot be assimilated into the logic of our world. In the incarnation, God eludes our grasp and subverts our systems of meaning from within. God is 'the breaking in on us of what is wholly unmasterable.'

Williams is of course no Marcionite. He acknowledges that Christ is not really an alien darkness: he is the light of the world. But this light is disturbing, since it interrupts our blindness and complacency. It produces 'a kind of vertigo; it makes me a stranger to myself, to everything I have ever taken for granted.' Christ is light, but we are traumatized when the light pierces our protective shield. In the aftermath of this shining, we find that our identity, our internal coherence, has come undone. Our religious language is shipwrecked on Christ. We are the wounded survivors of the advent of God, compelled now to find new ways of making sense of reality. 'I have to find a new way of knowing myself, identifying myself, uttering myself, talking of myself, imaging myself.' God's light has blinded us – not because God is darkness, but because our eyes are so dim. 'When God's light breaks on my darkness,' Williams writes, 'the first thing I know is that I don't know, and never did.'

The divine interruption thus cuts right to the core of human language, just as, in psychoanalysis, the childhood trauma strikes at the core of the self. As in the story of Babel, the resurrection produces a confusion of tongues, a scattering of our ways of relating and our capacity to make meaning. God 'confuses the whole of my speech and imagery.' Our religious language tries to bring God under control, to assimilate God within our ready-made systems of meaning, to turn God into a reassuring projection of our

---

[9] The quotations that follow are from 'A Ray of Darkness,' preached in the early 1980s and published in *A Ray of Darkness: Sermons and Reflections* (Cambridge, MA: Cowley, 1994).

own needs and desires. Such religious language is a barrier against God's strangeness: that is why God's attack on language is launched primarily against the beachhead of human religiosity.

For Williams, then, hearing God's word – encountering God's *logos* in Jesus – is a sort of neurosis. Its symptoms can include 'sickness, ecstasy, madness, intuition, speechlessness.' It induces something akin to schizophrenia, a tearing apart of whatever identity I had constructed for myself, a jarring dislocation of the systems of meaning by which I gain control over my world. 'Whatever makes the world new and makes me strange to myself, . . . this is God.' This unsettling account of God and language might be read as an extended commentary on MacKinnon's lapidary proposition (adapted from Euripides): 'Whom God wills to save, he first drives mad.'[10]

There is an immense shadow lurking in the background here, which I have neglected to mention till now. It is the Christian vision of the world as fallen – what Vladimir Lossky calls the 'nocturnal side' of creation.[11] Following Augustine, Williams sees original sin as an ugly wound running right through the middle of things, and most acutely through human reason and experience itself. This is not a moralistic obsession with individual vices but a universal vision of tragic disorder: the whole 'frame of things' has come disjointed.[12]

Anyone acquainted with theology today will know that this Augustinian vision has become unfashionable. We are too committed to moral agency and empowerment, or to the cultivation of virtues, or to human capacities to initiate social change: we are, in a word, Pelagians. More than almost any other contemporary thinker, Williams has resisted the deep undercurrent of Pelagianism in modern thought. Though he rarely speaks explicitly of 'sin,' his thought begins to make sense only against the backdrop of the doctrine of original sin, in something like its full Augustinian form. Indeed it is tempting to call this the negative source of Williams' theology, the dark star around which his thought silently orbits.

The importance of Augustine is foregrounded in Williams' first book, *The Wound of Knowledge*, written in his late twenties and

---

[10] Donald MacKinnon, *God the Living and the True* (Westminster: Dacre Press, 1940), 14.

[11] Vladimir Lossky, *The Mystical Theology of the Eastern Church* (London: James Clarke, 1957), 133.

[12] Shakespeare, *Macbeth*, 3.2.16.

published in 1979. Here, he finds in Augustine a unique awareness of 'the tragic, the senseless, the irremediable' dimensions of human experience.[13] Augustine saw the human self as a small point in a 'vast structure of forces' whose operation cannot easily be discerned by human reason. We imagine ourselves to be the real centre of things, when in fact 'human reality is acted upon at least as much as acting.' We tend to interpret everything around us as extensions of ourselves; we make our home in a house of mirrors, so that the whole world becomes a twisted reflection of our own desires. Because we are fallen, even our belief in God – *especially* that belief – cannot simply be trusted but must be scrutinized and subjected to a ruthless suspicion.

In a lecture on modern literature, T. S. Eliot once said that when the idea of original sin disappears from a culture, the representation of human beings tends to become more and more unreal, more dreamlike and 'vaporous.'[14] Augustinianism is realism. Its opposite is not a cheery human optimism, as is often thought, but a cruel and disabling unworldliness. Awareness that things are disordered – and that our own thinking is part of that disorder – keeps us morally alert, suspicious of easy certainties, attentive to the real tissue of human experience with all its tragic failings and uncertainties. For Williams, the only hope worth having is one that emerges from the 'doomed frailty' of every human hope. The only human story worth having is one pieced back together from 'the muddled and painful litter of experience.'

The death of Jesus shatters our religious confidence and overthrows our fantasies. In Jesus, we meet God not as someone safe and familiar but as a stranger. The cross, Williams says, is God's own negative theology, rendering impotent all our knowledge of God. An alarming silence now reigns right at the core of the human capacity to make and share meanings. God's incursion into history leaves a 'crater' in language, to borrow Karl Barth's famous wartime metaphor. Yet for Williams, none of this implies that human speech about God is merely crushed into silence. Instead, the trauma of Christ is the beginning of a new community, a new form of life, a new way of speaking about God in the presence of other human

---

[13] Rowan Williams, *The Wound of Knowledge: Christian Spirituality from the New Testament to St. John of the Cross* [1979] (2nd ed.; London: Darton, Longman & Todd, 1990), Chapter 4.

[14] T. S. Eliot, *After Strange Gods: A Primer of Modern Heresy* (London: Faber & Faber, 1934), 42.

lives. Language is annihilated by the trauma of Christ, but it is also born anew. From the silence of Holy Saturday there emerges a new community whose vocabulary has been 'shattered and re-formed.' This community has to begin the slow work of reshaping its language, 'subverting and reconstructing other traditions and vocabularies' as it tries to make sense of the world into which Christ has risen.[15] The Christian tradition as a whole, Williams argues, is this continuing process of the conversion of human language to God.

According to the later Wittgenstein, philosophy is a therapeutic endeavour: 'Work on philosophy . . . is really more work on oneself. On one's own conception. On how one sees things.'[16] In the same way, if Christ is a wound then theology is a sort of therapeutics of Christian identity, an attempt to unmask our fantasies and expose us to reality. Theology, as Williams also learned from Wittgenstein, is not really about ideas but about *life*. Through Christ's resurrection, the reality of God has become woven into the fabric of human experience. God is what fractures our identity, and God is the new coherence of our stories. To perform this coherence, to make God's reality legible in the embodied pattern of our lives, is what it means to speak of God. Simply put, 'to live the forgiven life wholeheartedly *is* . . . to speak of God.'[17]

When Milton's Adam awakens for the first time in paradise, he looks about him and erupts into bewildered praise:

Tell me, how may I know him, how adore,
From whom I have that thus I move and live,
And feel that I am happier than I know.[18]

Adam is shocked into speech. And that is what theology is like: a shock of awareness, a stunned stammering as we awaken to the surprising advent of the second Adam, the Word, God's own startling speech in our world.

---

[15] Williams, 'A Ray of Darkness,' 102.

[16] Ludwig Wittgenstein, *Culture and Value* (Oxford: Blackwell, 1980), 24.

[17] Williams, *Resurrection*, 87.

[18] John Milton, *Paradise Lost*, 8.280–82.

4

Boundaries

Past the dismantled door:
dust and linen on the floor.[1]

Christ's resurrection, then, is hardly a source of edification and consolation: it is a wound, a trauma that strikes at the roots of human identity. When the women get to the empty tomb, they flee in shock, 'for terror and amazement had seized them, and they said nothing to anyone, for they were afraid' (Mk 16.8). The resurrection causes a tectonic upheaval in the landscape of human community. This earthquake is the beginning of the church, and the church's subsequent history is a series of tenuous attempts to make sense of its traumatic beginning. Yet trauma is, by definition, something that cannot be fully integrated into a person's experience; and in the same way, the resurrection remains a sensitive wound, something unstable and disruptive right at the centre of Christian identity. Indeed Christ's presence in the church is always hidden, strange, and unsettling. If there is real continuity between the church and Christ, it is the continuity between a wound and a surgeon's scalpel. The church is that traumatized community which God's intervention has left in the world – a wound for the world's healing.

In one of his poems, Williams describes the 'bored and pious' air with which trained ecclesiastics calmly intone about the mystery of the resurrection.[2] Much of his writing from the 1970s and 1980s forms a protest against such pious boredom. His approach is closer to that of Graham Greene's decrepit whisky priest, who sees Christ's

---

[1] Rowan Williams, 'Carol,' in *Headwaters* (Oxford: Perpetua Press, 2008), 27.
[2] Rowan Williams, 'Great Sabbath,' in *The Poems of Rowan Williams* (Grand Rapids: Eerdmans, 2002).

resurrection as something dark and threatening, a terror from which we try to protect ourselves:

> 'Oh,' the priest said, 'that's another thing altogether – God *is* love . . . . We wouldn't recognize *that* love. It might even look like hate. It would be enough to scare us – God's love. It set fire to a bush in the desert, didn't it, and smashed open graves and set the dead walking in the dark. Oh, a man like me would run a mile to get away if he felt that love around.'[3]

In classical Greek theology, Christ is said to take on our human nature in order to make it whole. 'Whatever is not assumed is not healed,' according to Gregory of Nazianzus. That is how Williams sees it too, except that he identifies humanness not with any substantial 'nature' but with the whole world of language, mediation, and social exchange. In Christ, human sociality is crucified and resurrected, judged and redeemed. What the resurrection produces then is not an ideal or perfected human society – not utopia – but a real flesh-and-blood community marked as much by failure as by success. Yet it is a community in which all the normal human boundaries have been decisively altered. The whole shape of what is possible for human life has changed; the barriers have come down.

The resurrection, Williams argues, is a universal happening. For Christ, creation has no frontiers. And the existence of the church is already implicated in the existence of the risen Christ: the resurrection immediately gives rise to a new community whose imagination has been converted to this new and unbounded world, the 'new creation' of the gospel (Gal. 6.15). The church exists not for itself but for the sake of a reconciled humanity. Indeed the church *is* humanity made new, a new world in which the old walls of division have been torn down.

Williams' vision here is shaped above all by the imaginative world of modern Russian Orthodoxy, where redemption is envisaged as the removal of boundaries and the creation of a new organic catholicity (*sobornost*). According to the nineteenth-century philosopher Vladimir Solovyov, God overcomes the

---

[3] Graham Greene, *The Power and the Glory* (Harmondsworth: Penguin, 1971), 199–200.

dark power by which humanity is fragmented into a chaos of 'anarchic multiplicity,' and salvation means 'the sanctification and renovation of the whole human essence,' the creation of unity in a broken world.[4] In a less speculative and philosophical form, Sergius Bulgakov also describes redemption as 'the removal of the limits of limited being,' so that a new human community comes to share in the limitless life of Christ. The church's universality, Bulgakov argues, is as wide as the universality of Christ, and therefore as wide as creation itself:

> The limits of the Church . . . coincide with the limits of the power of the Incarnation and Pentecost, but these limits *do not exist at all* . . . . The universe is the periphery, the cosmic face of the Church.[5]

Later in the twentieth century, Vladimir Lossky would similarly speak of salvation as 'the removal of an obstacle,' and the life of the church as boundless in its cosmic catholicity. In the resurrection, God 'breaks through' the barrier of death, so that there are no longer any boundaries that could divide creation into pieces. In this way, the risen Christ 'unifies' and 'sanctifies' all created being.[6] Williams echoes this Russian tradition – though in a rather demythologized form – when he depicts the resurrection as the creation of a new human community whose social boundaries are as wide as humanity.

For Williams, the resurrection brings forth new social patterns – forgiveness, peacemaking, patience, truth-telling – which overcome whatever barriers had previously been in force. And this new form of social life entails new ways of speaking about God. In Wittgensteinian terms, redemption is the creation of a new form of life and a new shared language. As Williams has said more recently:

> We learn to look at all human faces with the rather disturbing knowledge that they are faces that God has already looked at . . . . Any divisions in our world, class, race, church loyalty, have to

---

[4] Vladimir Solovyov, *Russia and the Universal Church* [1889] (London: Geoffrey Bles, 1948), 150–53, 180.

[5] Sergius Bulgakov, *The Bride of the Lamb* [1945], trans. Boris Jakim (Grand Rapids: Eerdmans, 2002), 266–67.

[6] Vladimir Lossky, *The Mystical Theology of the Eastern Church* (London: James Clarke, 1957), 135–37.

be confronted with the painful truth that apparently we find it easier than God does to manage without certain bits of the human creation.[7]

The resurrection is God's unequivocal 'Yes' to all the diverse bits of humanity; it is God's commitment to a reconciled world. This is why, as Williams has often argued, the first-century Christians perceived questions of social identity and social boundaries as *theological* questions, questions about the identity of God.

Redemption, therefore, is never a matter of private 'spiritual' salvation, nor is it a vaguely edifying symbol of human striving for life and justice. It is, rather, an embodied occurrence within our world, something that changes what is possible for all human lives. The resurrection alters the world at its deepest level; that is what the early Christians recognized when they said that one particular human life had become the foundation of the cosmos (Jn 1.1-5). If the resurrection creates a new community which is universal in scope, from here it is only a small step to viewing the significance of Jesus as parallel to the act of creation itself. The 'generative' character of the resurrection 'is as radical as the generative significance of our language about the world's source and context, God.'[8] It is possible to speak of the universal scope of the resurrection only by articulating a cosmic vision – what Christians call 'creation.' Again here Williams remains close to modern Russian thought. It is no accident that Bulgakov's system includes the doctrine of creation not as a separate topic but as one branch of ecclesiology; the boundaries of creation are identical with the boundaries of the church.[9]

Through the resurrection, the world has been fundamentally reordered in relation to Jesus. His life cannot be described as though it belonged to just one partition of reality. There is no corner of human experience from which he is absent. Thus Williams insists, rather unfashionably, on the importance of the empty tomb and on the physical embodiment of the risen Christ. If Christ is not

---

[7] Rowan Williams, *Ponder These Things: Praying with Icons of the Virgin* (Norwich: Canterbury Press, 2002), 72.

[8] Rowan Williams, 'Trinity and Revelation' [1986], in *On Christian Theology* (Oxford: Blackwell, 2000), 138.

[9] Bulgakov, *The Bride of the Lamb.*

raised in bodily form, then he would remain foreign to embodied human experience, to all those awkward joys and sorrows of social existence. It is *bodily* resurrection that secures Christ's relevance to our lives here and now.

Williams even suggests that christological thinking – that is, reflection on Christ's identity – emerges from those new patterns of social life which we call 'church.' It was the drastic reordering of human relations that compelled the early Christians to speak of the divinity of Jesus. Christians simply find themselves unable to speak of God without telling Jesus' story. Jesus has entered into the very definition of God through his impact on the life of a human community. 'Nothing is more fundamental than Jesus, nothing will bring us closer to the heart of being itself than Jesus.'[10] As Donald MacKinnon had also argued, the resurrection is the 'projection of a raw piece of human history' as a happening of universal importance, so that one event discloses the secret of creation and of God's relation to all creatures.[11]

From that bloody scrap of history, the whole world is now transfigured with meaning. As T. S. Eliot writes in *The Rock*:

A moment in time but time was made through that moment: for without the meaning there is no time, and that moment of time gave the meaning.

Because of the resurrection, Christ is alive, active, universally available. God now looks at all things – all human beings, all history, all creation – through one small window: Jesus of Nazareth, the slain victim and glorified *logos* of history.

---

[10] Rowan Williams, *The Dwelling of the Light: Praying with Icons of Christ* (Norwich: Canterbury Press, 2003), 71.

[11] Donald MacKinnon, 'Atonement and Tragedy,' in *Borderlands of Theology and Other Essays* (Philadelphia: J. B. Lippincott, 1968), 102–3.

5

Tradition

Your histories belong to me here.[1]

A divinity student at Oxford or Cambridge in the 1980s could have been forgiven for supposing that early Christian history is really just one damned thing after another. British academic theology at the time was dominated by a profound scepticism towards doctrinal tradition, coupled with an implicit trust in the primacy of modern reason. One of the leading Christian historians at the time, the Oxford scholar Maurice Wiles, advocated a method of 'doctrinal criticism,' whereby the early faith of the church is carefully extricated from its outdated metaphysical framework. Doctrine remains valid, but only after it has been recast in a form that fits the scientific, anti-supernatural worldview of modern thought. Like many scholars of his generation, Wiles believed that the really great figures of Christian history are those maligned and misunderstood characters, the heretics – hence Wiles's own absorbing interest in the thought of Arius, the archetypal heretic of the fourth century.

As a young lecturer at Cambridge and Oxford in the 1980s, Rowan Williams had a quite different perception of the continuing vitality of Christian tradition. Compared to colleagues like Maurice Wiles, he viewed the history of Christian thought with a remarkable theological confidence. His decade-long immersion in the world of Russian Orthodoxy had done its work: he would now never be able to look at the Christian tradition as a merely secular affair, would never be able to accept the procedure of doctrinal criticism with its easy division between the enlightened methods of modern thought and the antiquated world of early Christian dogma.

---

[1] Rowan Williams, 'Twelfth Night' (I), in *The Poems of Rowan Williams* (Grand Rapids: Eerdmans, 2002), 41.

Vladimir Lossky had criticized the habit of studying church history with methods that bracket out the factor which is, in fact, most essential to the church – its religious nature. Where this occurs, Lossky argued, the religious dimension is merely replaced by something else, such as social or political interests: 'We think ourselves shrewder, more up to date, in invoking these factors as the true guiding forces of ecclesiastical history.'[2] In contrast, Lossky defined tradition as the critical memory of the church, made alive by the Holy Spirit.[3] Nothing could have been further from the spirit of 1980s British theology than such an assumption that the 'true guiding forces' of doctrinal history might be theological realities – that church history is part of 'the story of redemption,' as Georges Florovsky put it.[4] But Williams accepted exactly this assumption, and throughout the 1980s he set about developing a full-scale assault on the methods of doctrinal criticism, together with an expansive theological reinterpretation of the development of heresy and orthodoxy in the fourth and fifth centuries. Not that he was ever personally hostile towards colleagues like Wiles. But their whole approach to historical scholarship prompted him to try to show that church history can be understood theologically. 'Church history as a spiritual discipline'[5]: that was Williams' response to the cool rationalism of doctrinal criticism.

Williams argues that the church has always been faced with the task of negotiating its own continuity with the past. In the second century, this is attested in the development of various 'rules of faith.' The striking thing about these early doctrinal affirmations, Williams notes, is their extraordinary fragility. A community generated by a traumatic event of rupture must try 'to explain how it locates itself in a world decisively disrupted and contradicted.' Thus, the struggle for a normative Christianity, an 'orthodoxy,' belongs to the essence of Christian community. Orthodoxy is the church's attempt

[2] Vladimir Lossky, *The Mystical Theology of the Eastern Church* (London: James Clarke, 1957), 13.

[3] Vladimir Lossky, 'Tradition and Traditions,' *In the Image and Likeness of God* (Crestwood, NY: St Vladimir's Seminary Press, 1974), 156.

[4] Georges Florovsky, 'Revelation and Interpretation,' in *Collected Works of Georges Florovsky* (Belmont: Nordland, 1972), I, 26.

[5] Rowan Williams, *Why Study the Past?* (Grand Rapids: Eerdmans, 2005), 110.

to resist fragmentation and to compose for itself a coherent social imaginary.[6]

If the Christian community is a theological reality, the beginning of a new reconciled humanity, then the church's history will be a matter of urgent theological importance for the present. For Williams, good historical writing is writing 'that constructs that sense of who we are by a real engagement with the strangeness of the past,' so that our present identity is seen to be bound up with things that are no longer easy for us to grasp. The purpose of historical study is to invite us into 'a process of questioning and being questioned by the past,' so that we come to see that the Christian past is right at the centre of the Christian present.[7] The present is simply what the past is doing now.

Williams' most important contribution to the study of doctrinal history is his influential 1987 work, *Arius: Heresy and Tradition*.[8] Here, he argues that the Arian controversy was essentially a series of debates about the nature of Christian continuity. How does the church remain faithful in a new historical situation? Should the church simply remain committed to the language and formulations of the past? Or is some kind of innovation necessary in order to secure a deeper continuity? An axiom of modern writing on heresy is, as Jacques Berlinerblau has wryly observed, 'the belief that the heretic is a progressive element, one who heroically ... expands the parameters of a restricted conscience collective for future generations to benefit.'[9] Against this trend, Williams depicts Arius as 'a committed theological conservative.'[10] In his account, Arius emerges not only as the archetypal heretic, but also as an archetypal conservative who viewed himself as a guardian of Christian formulae, standing firm against the threatening encroachment of the Nicene innovators. Arius presented himself both as a biblical exegete and as a defender of doctrinal tradition. The whole Arian

---

[6] Rowan Williams, 'Defining Heresy,' in *The Origins of Christendom in the West*, ed. Alan Kreider (Edinburgh: T&T Clark, 2001), 324–27.

[7] Williams, *Why Study the Past*, 23–24, 28.

[8] Rowan Williams, *Arius: Heresy and Tradition* [1987] (2nd ed.; London: SCM, 2001).

[9] Jacques Berlinerblau, 'Toward a Sociology of Heresy, Orthodoxy, and *Doxa*,' *History of Religions* 40 (2001), 344.

[10] Williams, *Arius*, 175.

controversy, Williams argues, is thus a series of debates about 'how to be loyal to a tradition under strain,'[11] how to remain faithful to the biblical testimony amid the changed conditions of the fourth century.

In contrast to Arius's staunch attachment to traditional language, it was the genius of Athanasius to perceive that continuity with tradition can demand a break in linguistic continuity. Athanasius realized that there can be no question of a simple choice between conservation and innovation. The question posed to the church, rather, was 'what *kind* of innovation would best serve the integrity of the faith handed down,' since the continuity of Christian belief involves much more than the mere repetition of traditional vocabulary. In short, then, the Nicene prelates reluctantly adopted fresh language only in order to hold fast to a belief that had been threatened by the archaic repetition of traditional language. Williams thus argues that the theology of Nicaea represents a crucial moment in doctrinal history, when the church perceived that critical theological reflection is not only legitimate but necessary:

> The loyal and uncritical repetition of formulae is seen to be inadequate as a means of securing continuity at anything more than a formal level; Scripture and tradition require to be read in a way that brings out their strangeness, their non-obvious and non-contemporary qualities, in order that they may be read both freshly and truthfully from one generation to another. They need to be made more *difficult* before we can accurately grasp their simplicities . . . . And this 'making difficult,' this confession that what the gospel says in Scripture and tradition does not instantly and effortlessly make sense, is perhaps one of the most fundamental tasks for theology.[12]

Here, Williams compares the Nicene crisis with the German Church Struggle of the 1930s, where a small group of pastors and teachers resisted the German church's acceptance of Nazi ideology. The Barmen Declaration, written by Karl Barth and other 'confessing' leaders, represents not a confessional conservatism but a profound

---

[11] Rowan Williams, 'Baptism and the Arian Controversy,' in *Arianism after Arius*, ed. Michel R. Barnes and Daniel H. Williams (Edinburgh: T&T Clark, 1993), 177.

[12] Williams, *Arius*, 235–36.

struggle for theological self-awareness and for a new openness to the church's originating event, so that the gospel becomes at once more difficult and more immediate in its contemporary demands. The lesson of Barmen, Williams thinks, is that 'proclaiming *now* the same gospel as before is a great deal less easy than it sounds.' It is a matter of intense struggle, of risk and commitment. At both Barmen and Nicaea, the problem is to identify the kinds of changes necessary in order to secure a proper continuity with the past. And this will always require a critical and creative re-engagement with the past.

Indeed, Williams argues that only orthodoxy can free us for a properly critical stance towards the past. Here he has an eye on the faux radicalism of his Cambridge colleague Don Cupitt and others like him who see a zero-sum game between a received tradition and present faithfulness. 'Only tradition makes thinking possible – an engagement, even a struggle, with what is given, rather than a passive and meaningless observation. Paradoxically, it is only "orthodoxies" . . . that enable us to ask questions.'[13]

The history of doctrine is, then, a history of formative conflicts and struggles. In a Wittgensteinian key, Williams argues that there is no pure doctrinal meaning which could be abstracted from these historical situations. 'What the articulation of doctrinal truth concretely *is* can be traced only through the detailed reworking and re-imagining of its formative conflicts.'[14] So it would be a mistake to think of conflict as a clash between truth and error, or between a pre-existing 'orthodoxy' and a divergent 'heresy.' On the contrary, orthodoxy comes into being only through its struggle with heresy: it does not pre-exist that struggle but emerges from it. The language of Nicaea *became* orthodox because it found a new way of preserving faithfulness to the Christian past in a changed world.

Williams' historical work from the 1980s is thus at pains to underscore the unfinished character of doctrinal orthodoxy. The production of authentic continuity with the past is always a new task and challenge. As the Arian controversy so vividly illustrates, there is no straightforward 'deposit of faith' which needs only to be conserved and defended. Rather, orthodoxy must be experienced as something still future, a continuing project, which is not yet finally

---

[13] Rowan Williams, 'What Is Catholic Orthodoxy?' in *Essays Catholic and Radical*, ed. Rowan Williams and Kenneth Leech (London: Bowerdean Press, 1983), 12.

[14] Williams, *Arius*, 25.

settled or resolved. The task of Christian theology is to take up the project of traditioning the past, generating new forms of continuity so that the past appears not merely as history but as *tradition*, a living resource which enables faithfulness in the present. Orthodoxy then is not so much a settled system of beliefs as a 'tool,' a set of self-reflective practices, 'a tradition of discriminating, imaging and symbolising.' It is the church's therapeutic response to the trauma of Christ's resurrection. The church remains orthodox only to the extent that it remains attentive and answerable to that universal event which lies at the origin of its life.

Conversely, 'heresies' are those options in doctrinal history which sever the church from the universality of Christ, and so limit the range of Christian imagination. Heresy is an impoverishment of the church's language. In the Arian system, the difficulties of traditional concepts were ironed out, and basic doctrinal themes (such as divine freedom, transcendence, and incomprehensibility) were pressed to their extreme logical conclusions. Arianism was not a complete deviation from orthodoxy – its basic premises were rooted in tradition – but was a failure of nerve, an inability to accept the incompleteness and ambiguity of Christian belief. Its 'heretical' impulse lay in what Williams calls a 'destructive longing for final clarity, totality of vision' – the same totalizing impulse that 'brings forth the monsters of religious and political idolatry.'[15]

Orthodoxy, for its part, also seeks a sort of comprehensiveness. But instead of pursuing a total vision that eliminates ambiguity, it aims to provide a context which is flexible enough to accommodate the real complexities of Christian belief and practice. Here again Williams remains a good Wittgensteinian: 'What's ragged should be left ragged.'[16] The comprehensiveness of orthodoxy lies not in any conceptual tidiness but in a constantly expanding network of interpretive resources in which the 'raggedness' of Christian language is retained. Orthodoxy is messy, like real life.

In principle, of course, there is no way to predict in advance what heresy might look like, or how it might differ from some future orthodoxy. This question can never be settled: that is Williams' point. There must be continual negotiation and dispute over the

---

[15] Williams, 'Catholic Orthodoxy,' 25.

[16] Ludwig Wittgenstein, *Culture and Value* (Chicago: University of Chicago Press, 1980), 45.

church's identity; at every stage of the church's journey, the gospel needs to become stranger and more difficult.

Karl Barth once said that Christian doctrine is truthful only to the extent that it 'points beyond itself and summons us to hear not itself, but [Christ].'[17] The Christian tradition, in Williams' view, is the extension through time of that act of self-dispossessing witness. Tradition is a theological reality. It is not meant to answer all our questions; its aim is to point beyond itself, to formalize its own unfinishedness, to hold open a space for new encounters with what Flannery O'Connor called God's 'dark and disruptive' grace.[18] Tradition keeps the church in contact with its own traumatic origins: the dark grace of an empty tomb.

---

[17] Karl Barth, *Church Dogmatics* IV/3 (London: T&T Clark, 2009), 419.

[18] Flannery O'Connor, 'The Catholic Novelist in the Protestant South,' in *Mystery and Manners: Occasional Prose* (New York: Farrar, Straus & Giroux, 1969).

6

Growth

We test the feel of an unyielding difficulty,
not yet sure.[1]

Edith Wharton said that other people are like estates: we know of them only what abuts our own. Can persons who are different ever really know one another? Is there an absolute difference between us, ruling out any real understanding and engagement? Or is difference a temporary obstacle that can eventually be overcome? In 1992, Williams left academic life and was consecrated Bishop of Monmouth; now he could put his thinking about the church to the test. In the years that followed, he had ample opportunity to experience the way human beings are divided by seemingly intractable differences; such experiences of division troubled him deeply and left permanent marks on his theological thinking.

I have been exploring Williams' commitment to a catholic understanding of Christ and humanity: Christ as the beginning of a reconciled human community in which all dividing boundaries are broken down. Williams' work as a church leader has been one long struggle to uphold this catholic vision. It is a vision that sharpens the riddle of identity and difference. If there is an absolute difference between persons, then there can be no genuinely catholic community, only a conglomerate of individuals who occasionally bump up against each other in more or less bewildered incomprehension. Or if the difference between persons finally collapses, then again there is no catholic community, but only a colourless homogeneity, more like the society of Huxley's *Brave New World* than like the glorious clamour of a family comprising

---

[1] Rowan Williams, 'Winterreise: For Gillian Rose, 9 December 1995,' in *The Poems of Rowan Williams* (Grand Rapids: Eerdmans, 2002), 84.

every tribe and tongue. A catholic conception of human sociality demands that both doctrines – absolute difference and fundamental sameness – be firmly refused. Williams instead has groped towards a third way, in which difference is neither absolutized nor abolished, but tenuously preserved; my own identity emerges from the hard work of sustaining the difference between myself and others.

Throughout the 1990s, Williams returns again and again to this problem of the relation between identity and difference. In the early 1990s, he found a tool that let him solve the puzzle: that tool was the philosophy of Hegel, and Williams' discovery of Hegel marks one of the most important turning points in his intellectual career. It was Hegel who helped him to see identity and difference not as stark alternatives but as mutually constituting realities.

In an early essay on Donald MacKinnon's theology,[2] Williams still found it possible to rehearse the usual textbook criticisms of Hegelianism. Hegel's God is a totalizing principle that reconciles all opposites into itself. All differences collapse into a sublime and idolatrous whole, a unity beyond differentiation. The contingency and limitations of human history are obliterated in this schema, as thesis and antithesis drive relentlessly towards a higher synthesis. Hegelianism leaves no room for what is ambiguous and unresolved in our experience, the 'tragic limitedness' of human history.

That was Williams in 1986, reflecting not only MacKinnon's influence but also an aversion to some of the rather imperious varieties of Hegelianism that he had encountered in nineteenth-century Russian theology. By 1995, however, he would disavow these criticisms of Hegel.[3] Why the change of heart? In 1991, a personal experience would radically alter his appreciation of Hegel: at a conference in Cambridge, he met the Jewish philosopher Gillian Rose, one of Hegel's most vigorous and eccentric contemporary interpreters, and they had soon formed an unlikely friendship. Rose died in 1995, and by then her friendship with Williams had left indelible marks on his imaginative life. The aim of Rose's philosophy was to wrest Hegel from his teleological interpreters,

---

[2] Rowan Williams, 'Trinity and Ontology' [1986], in *On Christian Theology* (Oxford: Blackwell, 2000).

[3] Rowan Williams, 'Between Politics and Metaphysics: Reflections in the Wake of Gillian Rose' [1995], in *Wrestling with Angels*, ed. Mike Higton (Grand Rapids: Eerdmans, 2007), 76 note 37.

to show that he is a thinker not of synthesis but of opposition. Her writing, ruthlessly exacting and starkly evocative, sets out to shatter not only teleology but also its contemporary alternative, the French postmodern ethics of 'the Other.' In French theory, exemplified by Emmanuel Levinas, the self must be 'devastated, traumatised, unthroned, by the commandment to substitute the other for itself.' The two options in contemporary thought – teleological loss of difference and ethical loss of self – are, Rose argues, really two sides of the same coin. They are evasions of the world's brokenness and of the intractable difficulty of living with differences in a damaged world. We betray difference whenever we try to 'mend the world,'[4] whether through a secular or religious teleology or through the elevation of an absolutely transcendent Other.

Rose argues that instead of seeking resolution, as though difference were an obstacle to be overcome, we ought to accept the flawed 'middle' between every difference and to work at sustaining this broken middle. This is what Rose calls the 'agon' of difference,[5] where we endure the anxiety of difference without seeking the relief of synthesis. Here we neither grudgingly evade opposition nor blindly accede to it, but willingly act in the face of an opposition which can never be overcome. As Hegel put it, we need to 'tarry with the negative.' My own position is already vulnerable and bound to fail; yet by staking a position, it becomes possible to negotiate difference and so to be changed. Already knowing that I will fail, I nevertheless stake myself again.

Rose's interpretation of Hegel might be read as a philosophy of growth, an account of the way change emerges when the tragic limitations of our experience are sustained. It is this brand of Hegelianism, stringently ethical and anti-teleological, that became central to Williams' thought in the 1990s. It gave him a precise way of articulating the irresolvable tragic dimensions of social life and a way of understanding the significance of the church as the adumbration of a new catholic – that is to say, a fully human – community. Thus in a series of essays,[6] Williams took up Rose's Hegelianism and

---

[4] Gillian Rose, *The Broken Middle* (Oxford: Blackwell, 1992), 293.

[5] Rose, *Broken Middle*, 296.

[6] His major studies are 'Hegel and the Gods of Postmodernity' (1992), 'Between Politics and Metaphysics: Reflections in the Wake of Gillian Rose' (1995); and 'Logic and Spirit in Hegel' (1998); together with the deeply Hegelian analysis of 'Balthasar and

transmuted it into a Christian theology of identity, difference, and sociality. Following Rose's polemic against French postmodernism, he argues that difference is neither absolute nor ultimately reducible to sameness; difference must be endured, never resolved. Hegel's dialectic, Williams argues, 'is meant to challenge the all-sufficiency of the polarity of simple identity and simple difference.'[7] If my identity is mediated to me through confrontation with another, then otherness and identity must be said to emerge dialectically, instead of being fixed in advance of personal encounter. Identity and otherness are mutually dependent and mutually mediating. Identity is constituted by relation; there is no such thing as pure identity, just as there is no such thing as absolute otherness.

It is very odd that Williams is so often mistaken for a thinker of postmodern sensibilities. Even if he has occasionally flirted with minor themes from Derrida and Levinas, he is deeply uneasy about the direction of French theory; by the early 1990s, Rose's potent Hegelianism had effectively vaccinated Williams against *différance*. When he insists that language is always open-ended and incomplete, this has nothing to do with Derrida's notion of the infinite deferral of meaning; instead it is a Hegelian conception of the social mediation of truth.[8]

Authentic social exchange occurs wherever different persons mediate meaning to one another. Just think of the way understanding emerges from conversation: in a good conversation, something new appears which is not reducible to any of the individual speakers. For Williams, truth is that new thing that springs into being when different selves engage in the hard work of sustaining their differences. Openness to truth, therefore, is an experience of dispossession. We must give up our desire to possess the truth, in order to receive it and share it freely with others. What Williams calls 'negotiation' is this dynamism of giving and receiving. The self rebounds back to me when I give it freely, and the rebounded self is clearer, sharper, more definite than the self I gave away.

Difference' (1998). These are all collected in Mike Higton's edited volume, *Wrestling with Angels.*

[7] Williams, 'Hegel and the Gods of Postmodernity,' 29.

[8] Strangely, even Rose herself has occasionally been read as a thinker of Derridean sensibilities, in spite of the fact that her entire philosophical project was intended as a defiant critique of French postmodernism.

But this process of negotiation, this giving and receiving of the self, has a tragic shadow. The distance between myself and another is never overcome but only reasserted and sustained. There is no final harmony of shared truth, no synthesis, but only a slow limping history of dispossession and negotiation. Truthfulness is a risky venture. Above all else it demands patience, the refusal of any anaesthetic against the 'agon' of truth. Patience is never a sedate acceptance of things as they are but a costly commitment to endure unresolved difficulty, vulnerability, and loss. Human subjectivity is a continuing process of learning, a never-ending 'adjustment' of each self in relation to others.

Williams thus interprets all social life under the theological category of kenosis. He understands kenosis not as a divestment of the self to make way for a transcendent Other, but as a willingness to tarry with the negative, to undertake the painful work of negotiating difference. Williams insists that we must resist the desire to mend the tragic quality of human relationships. We cannot erase our identity, but we can relinquish the perverse desire to control, to force a resolution by overcoming the distance between ourselves and others. To return to Rose's language, kenosis is a willingness to endure the devastation of the 'middle.' It is not a matter of passivity, therefore, but of work – the hard, patient labour of life together.

There are, Williams thinks, no shortcuts to the slow formation of mutual subjectivity. There is no point attempting, with Levinas, a 'total self-cancellation before the sacredness of the Other.'[9] That would mean another person had encountered me as a mystical abyss rather than as an opportunity for mutual discovery, adjustment, and growth. Whether we try to bridge human distance through control or through self-erasure, the result is the same: an abortive dissolution of difference. Immature and destructive patterns of relating are those in which I fail to see others in their own proper distinctiveness, or to see how my own identity will need to be adjusted in relation to others. Wherever such failures occur, we obscure the gospel's promise of a new catholic humanity.

Williams' theology of the church is thus, at its heart, a theology of growth. For him, the gospel itself is at stake in the question whether the church is the venue of a continuing movement of human persons towards God and towards one another. Augustine described the

---

[9] Williams, 'Between Politics and Metaphysics,' 70.

church as 'a school' in which God is the teacher: 'in this school we are learning every day.'[10] Like Augustine, Williams places limited trust in sudden conversions and quick resolutions; one cannot live by such experiences. It is not the quick transformation of the self but the slow growth into maturity that really matters. The Christian life is comparable to nothing so much as an education, in which we progress by small daily increments. Christian spirituality is 'an education in the new humanity.'[11] Williams' sharpest criticism of Karl Barth springs from this educational vision of the Christian life. Barth's view of unilateral divine intervention fails to account for 'human growth, human diversity, and human freedom of response.' Barth is interested only in the way God speaks to us, not in the way we learn to hear and appropriate what is said.[12]

There is a sober realism in this picture of the church as a social order whose members represent vastly different stages of understanding, maturity, and responsiveness. There are persons whose participation in the visible ritual life of the church is very minimal, but who are still located somewhere on the spectrum of growth into human maturity before God. While the 'centre' of the church's ritual or hierarchical life is presumed to be normative in most ecclesiologies, Williams' theology is concerned with those who inhabit the fringes of the Christian community – those who need neither a sudden transformation nor a confronting call to discipleship, but only a continuation of growth by small, even imperceptible, degrees. One does not have to be near the centre; there is healing even in the hem of Christ's garment.

In Williams' thought, this conception of growth and patience is fused with MacKinnon's tragic emphasis. Like Gillian Rose, Williams comes close to renouncing teleology altogether. Whatever Christian eschatology might mean, it cannot posit any final triumph over human imperfection and limitation. To eliminate tragedy would be to do away with the difference that makes us human. Although this pessimistic note is seldom muted, its counterpoint in Williams' writing is a profound assurance that truthfulness is a real human possibility: possible because the structures of social life repose on

---

[10] Augustine, *Sermon* 16A.1.

[11] Rowan Williams, 'Against Anxiety, Beyond Triumphalism,' in *A Ray of Darkness: Sermons and Reflections* (Cambridge, MA: Cowley, 1994), 234.

[12] Rowan Williams, 'Barth on the Triune God' [1979], in *Wrestling with Angels*, 142.

an infinite depth of divine difference, divine self-donation, and divine truthfulness. Even the divine identity is constituted through difference: that is what the doctrine of the trinity means, and it is why Williams reads Hegel not as a philosopher external to the Christian tradition but as a thinker who elucidated the internal logic of Christian trinitarian faith.[13] While modern theologians tend to decry the influence of metaphysics in theological systems, Williams argues explicitly for a robust Hegelian metaphysics: 'We have for too long been sheepish about the theology in metaphysics and the metaphysics in theology.'[14] Thinking about God always entails thinking about human relations: that is the principle that Williams takes from the philosophy of Hegel. His reading of Hegel aims 'to abandon a theology-in-itself, a theology that refuses to be a way of thinking the nature of human sociality.'[15] Or more simply, he interprets Hegel's philosophy as catholic ecclesiology; he wants to show that speech about God is always simultaneously speech about a universal human community.

That was, of course, already the theme of Williams' earlier reflections on the resurrection: the existence of a catholic community is implicated in the existence of the risen one. When a rather gruff Donald MacKinnon reviewed Williams' 1982 book on *Resurrection*, he chided the author's tendency to indulge in 'imaginative sprawl' and 'to substitute reverie for hard analysis.'[16] It was the philosophy of Hegel that enabled Williams to move beyond 'reverie,' and to elaborate this theme with conceptual precision. But the broad outlines of his thought have not changed. A new human community – a community of difference, identity, and truthful subjectivity – is adumbrated in the redeemed sociality of the church.

This means the church will be a community marked by patience. It will look for its own identity as something not yet possessed. Here the church is sustained by what Sergius Bulgakov has called 'the patience of the Spirit.'[17] In the Holy Spirit, God is patient with

---

[13] Williams, 'Logic and Spirit in Hegel,' 48.

[14] Williams, 'Between Politics and Metaphysics,' 74.

[15] Williams, 'Logic and Spirit in Hegel,' 49.

[16] Donald MacKinnon, review of Rowan Williams, *Resurrection*, in *Scottish Journal of Theology* 36 (1983).

[17] Sergius Bulgakov, *The Comforter* [1936], trans. Boris Jakim (Grand Rapids: Eerdmans, 2004), 341.

us just as a parent is lovingly patient with the slow growth of a child. Indeed the Spirit *is* God's patience, God's own commitment to the slow process of growth and transformation, and to those fringe dwellers who remain remote from the church's visible centre.

In one of Iris Murdoch's fictional Socratic dialogues, Socrates cautions: 'Let's go slowly. In philosophy if you aren't moving at a snail's pace you aren't moving at all.'[18] For Williams, the same is often true of the Christian life: if we're not growing daily, almost imperceptibly, then we're not growing at all. Patience means endurance of hardship, a willingness to tarry with the experience of failure and incompleteness. But God does not stand aloof from our tragic experience; in the Holy Spirit, God bears our struggle and sustains it.

As Williams sees it, the church is the rough draft of a new humanity, and the Spirit is its author. Rough drafts are always a rather tragic state of affairs. But as every writer knows, there's only one thing to do about it, and that is to revise. That is the work of the Spirit: revising and repairing the human race, slowly and patiently, one fragment at a time.

---

[18] Iris Murdoch, 'Above the Gods: A Dialogue about Religion,' in *Existentialists and Mystics: Writings on Philosophy and Literature* (London: Chatto & Windus, 1997), 500.

7

Mission

Who can tell who might be
welcome here?[1]

The Welsh poet R. S. Thomas liked to speak of 'laboratories of
the spirit.' And the church, too, is a sort of laboratory. It is that
unbounded community in which Christ's resurrection has taken
effect, a place from which none of the raw materials of human
experience are excluded. The church is not an end in itself. It is
the experimental beginning of a new creation, what Williams calls
a 'pilot project for the human race.'[2] The church is God's own
experiment with a reconciled, catholic humanity. Catholicity is not
just one of the 'marks' of the church's identity; it is the church's
whole rationale, its form of life, its mode of encountering the world.
Catholicity is the continuing reality of the resurrection of Christ.

Augustine observed that the truth of Christ is demonstrated by
the sheer fact of Christian catholicity. The very word 'catholic,' he
said, testifies that Christ is risen: 'I would not believe the gospel
unless the authority of the church's catholicity moved me to do so.'[3]
In the same way, Williams thinks that the gospel is just the sort of
message that ought to take root in different places, languages, and
cultures, just the sort of thing that ought to be translatable into every
conceivable human situation. If the church were a parochial sect, its
own existence would disprove its message. A universal community,

---

[1] Rowan Williams, 'Kampala: The El Shaddai Coffee Bar,' in *The Poems of Rowan Williams* (Grand Rapids: Eerdmans, 2002), 71.

[2] Rowan Williams, 'The Church: God's Pilot Project,' an address to the Clergy Synod at Chelmsford, April 2006: http://www.archbishopofcanterbury.org/articles.php/1779/the-church-gods-pilot-project.

[3] Augustine, *Contra epistolam quam vocant fundamenti*, 5.

constantly reaching beyond itself to those from 'every tribe and
tongue and people and nation' (Rev. 5.9), shows that Christ is risen
indeed and that no human boundaries can contain his life.

The church's identity and its mission, therefore, are one and the
same. The church has no internal identity prior to its engagement
with the world. Its very existence is a demonstration that 'he is
not here; he is risen' (Lk. 24.6). Bearing witness to Christ is not
a secondary thing, not a mere application of the church's faith in
Christ; it is Christ's own life translated into the medium of human
community.

In Russian Orthodoxy, the catholicity of Christ is envisaged
in terms of cosmic ecclesiology. Eventually all reality will be
encompassed within the church; eventually everything will be
liturgy. Williams articulates the same universal vision, but from
the opposite standpoint: the church is not the goal of God's action,
not an end in itself, but only the beginning of a new world in the
midst of the old. He insists, therefore, that the church is not a
'special' form of sociality, but the place 'where the rationale of all
other relations is made plain.'[4] Christ enables a coherent mode of
human belonging in which all people draw their life from a common
well. 'The church is wider than the world,' said John Chrysostom.
Williams agrees: the message of Christ's resurrection continually
draws the church beyond itself, into a world whose lines of division
have been abolished. The catholicity of the church, therefore, is
simply its capacity 'to accommodate human beings in the full range
of their humanity.'[5]

Contemporary western societies have witnessed the emergence of
a new tribalism, fuelled by the logic of capitalism with its proliferation
of niche identities, and by the politics of multiculturalism with its
advocacy of mere 'difference' without any vision of a common good.
Such multicultural pluralism is a mirror image of the postmodern
ethics of difference, where each person is assumed to be absolutely
'other.' Once this doctrine of otherness has taken hold of political
imagination, Williams argues, we are left with the depressing
prospect of 'a world in which there aren't and couldn't be any real

---

[4] Rowan Williams, 'Incarnation and the Renewal of Community' [1989], in *On Christian Theology* (Oxford: Blackwell, 2000), 226.

[5] Rowan Williams, *A Margin of Silence: The Holy Spirit in Russian Orthodox Theology* (Québec: Éditions du Lys Vert, 2008), 43.

discussion of the goals and destiny of human beings as such.'[6] The resulting social order starts to look like a Hobbesian war of all against all, a chaotic rivalry between segregated interest groups, each ruthlessly brandishing its own rights and freedoms while the state is reduced to the role of suppressing open conflict by policing the borders of 'difference.'

This amounts to a crisis in our social imagination: we find ourselves unable to imagine what it might really mean to live together. Margaret Thatcher's prophecy has come true: there is no such thing (anymore) as society. Williams' thought in the 1990s was shaped by this social crisis. As Bishop of Monmouth and then Archbishop of Wales, he took on the role not only of pastor to the Christian community but also of a public witness to wider British society. In his scholarly writing in the 1990s, he struggled to articulate a distinctively political ecclesiology and to rethink the nature of contemporary society through the lens of Christian catholicity.

Drawing on the cosmic ecclesiology of Russian Orthodoxy, Williams projects Christian catholicity on to the screen of humanity as a whole. And again taking up the philosophy of Hegel, he tries to show that the church is not one interest group alongside others but a community whose only 'interest' is the interest of all. This is, after all, the distinctiveness of the Christian message. When the first disciples saw the risen one, their immediate response was to go away and testify: in meeting Christ ourselves, we discover something that serves not only our own good but the good of all. If Christ is anything less than the redeemer of the world, then it will not make sense to speak of him as our own 'personal lord and saviour.' He can be relevant to anybody only if he is relevant to all.

Here Williams develops Hegel's argument that there is no such thing as mere individual freedom; freedom is mediated through community, and any purely individual freedom is pathological. Human persons 'have no legitimate interests that are purely private or individual';[7] there are no legitimate individual ends which do not somehow coincide with the good of the whole community. Williams also explains the concept of 'rights' along these lines. Rights are

---

[6] Rowan Williams, *Mission and Christology* (J. C. Jones Memorial Lecture; Brynmawr: Church Missionary Society, Welsh Members' Council, 1994), 4–5.

[7] Rowan Williams, 'Logic and Spirit in Hegel' [1998], in *Wrestling with Angels*, ed. Mike Higton (Grand Rapids: Eerdmans, 2007), 44.

not something that I brandish like a weapon against the rights of others; rather I relinquish my purely private rights 'so as to negotiate with . . . other persons a good neither mine nor theirs.'[8] Wherever one social group is convinced of some particular right, it is their responsibility to enter into a wider process of negotiation in order to discover how their own aims can form part of a common good.

For Williams, then, real political engagement is a form of kenosis. Politics begins where I am dispossessed of my attachment to my own interests, and I accept responsibility for the interests of others. Gillian Rose had spoken of feminist politics in this way: she identified with its cause precisely because feminism seemed remote from her own needs and interests. Politics occurs not where each group lobbies for its own interests but where each pursues a wider vision of the social good – especially when private interests are not at stake. Supporting feminism, for Rose, becomes an act of political kenosis. Political action then is not a rivalry of private rights and freedoms but a patient and attentive re-envisioning of one's own aims in light of what is good for the whole society.

Such a political vision is, admittedly, addressed more to those in power than to the vulnerable and dispossessed, for whom the language of 'rights' and 'freedom' is often a last-ditch attempt to maintain a precarious footing within an oppressive social order. In the early 1980s, Williams was impressed by the emergence of Latin American liberation theology, with its vehement call for political action as a mode of Christian discipleship. Many western theologians imagined they could easily translate liberation theology into the domain of their own privileged world – hence the spectacle whereby a politics of liberation was transmuted into a fashionable 'method' for interpreting texts and traditions. Williams is too much of a realist to have been enticed by this kind of academic rhetoric. Instead his encounter with liberation theology provoked him to ask: what would it mean to practise Christian political commitment in a society like Britain, where the church is not a powerless or persecuted minority but is itself one of the institutions of cultural power?[9] While Christians in Latin America might rightly call for agency, empowerment, and drastic emergency measures, Williams

---

[8] Williams, 'Logic and Spirit,' 44.

[9] Rowan Williams, 'Liberation Theology and the Anglican Tradition,' in *Politics and Theological Identity: Two Anglican Essays* (London: Jubilee Group, 1984).

finds himself saying almost the opposite. In British society, where Anglicanism is established, the church's task is to give away power, to divest itself of security and privilege, to use its own voice to negotiate on behalf of more vulnerable social groups. It is a sort of liberation theology in reverse: a political theology articulated from above, rather than from below.

That was the whole point of Williams' controversial 2008 lecture on 'Civil and Religious Law in England.'[10] His remarks on Islamic sharia law were greeted with cries of alarm and incredulity: tabloid papers ran hysterical headlines about 'a victory for terrorists' or 'a victory for al Qaeda,' while one Home Office minister complained that Williams wanted Britain 'to fundamentally change the rule of law.' For a week or two, the whole world seemed to be clamouring for the Archbishop's resignation. But of course Williams was not trying to displace British law with Islamic law, nor to reduce all social orders to the same level, nor again merely to promote general sentiments of liberal broad-mindedness. He was, in fact, raising the simple Hegelian question: given that British society includes Muslim communities, is it possible to understand the ends of those communities as part of what is good for the whole society? How might the church – a community that still enjoys a lingering glow of cultural legitimacy – use its own cultural privilege to promote this process of the public negotiation of goods? Williams' aim was to model this Hegelian style of public engagement, where what is good for any single community becomes part of the vision of what is good for all.

Nothing could have more eloquently proved the importance of the Archbishop's lecture than the vociferous animosity of its reception. In a climate of deeply entrenched segregation, suspicion, and thinly veiled cultural hostility, his words were taken as an ominous threat – as though he had betrayed his own side in a culture war. But if Christ is risen and the church is catholic, then there can be no 'sides,' and the church's role is to dismantle the whole logic of side-taking. The church invites all members of society into a wider world, into a fully human community where the ends of each are identical with the ends of all. The real question is, 'can what *they* see be part of the

---

[10] Rowan Williams, 'Civil and Religious Law in England: A Religious Perspective,' 7 February 2008: http://www.archbishopofcanterbury.org/articles.php/1137/archbishops-lecture-civil-and-religious-law-in-england-a-religious-perspective.

world that I see?'[11] This is what Williams calls interactive pluralism, a form of social engagement in which distinctive communal loyalties are related to the wider society, resulting in greater social cohesion and a unity between the local and the universal. To articulate such an expansive and hospitable social vision is not a mere option. It is, he thinks, part of the church's vocation – its mission – to reach out across those boundaries that fragment the human community into self-protective ghettos. Strange as it might sound, the lecture on sharia law was, for Williams, simply part of what it means to say that Christ is risen.

In recent years, Williams' intensive involvement in Christian–Muslim dialogue – if all his recent lectures and essays on Islam were collected, they would form a sizable book – has been driven by the same understanding of Christian mission. Interfaith dialogue, he argues, is not an external activity on the part of the church. It is not a matter of politically correct inclusiveness or of liberal relativism: it is a matter of christology and of Christian faithfulness. It is a dimension of 'liturgy,' a public demonstration of the church's commitment to 'the finality of Christ.'[12] Far from relativizing the confession of the uniqueness of Christ, Williams sees 'the radical singleness of Jesus Christ' as the whole rationale for interfaith engagement.

Because Christ's life is catholic and unbounded, he is never fully absorbed by any particular human context. He is both 'native' and 'stranger' to all social locations.[13] The word of life and love that Christ addresses to the church is only the echo of a word addressed to the whole of humanity. As Vladimir Lossky argues, ecclesiology is derived from a vision of a redeemed humanity: the church's own 'internal' identity springs from its mission to embody a renewed creation.[14] The church itself has no good except the common good. Wherever it becomes withdrawn and introspective, the confession

---

[11] Rowan Williams, 'Christian Identity and Religious Plurality,' *The Ecumenical Review* 58:1 (2006), 73.

[12] Rowan Williams, 'The Finality of Christ in a Pluralist World,' a lecture in the Diocese of Guildford, March 2010: http://www.archbishopofcanterbury.org/articles.php/585/the-finality-of-christ-in-a-pluralist-world.

[13] Williams, *Mission and Christology*, 18.

[14] Vladimir Lossky, *The Mystical Theology of the Eastern Church* (London: James Clarke, 1957), 112–13.

of Christ withers. The life of Christ ceases to be available when we want it merely for ourselves; it is active only as we are pushed beyond ourselves into mission.

So Williams thinks the traditional language of 'mission' provides a unique way of articulating the place of the church in contemporary pluralist societies. Through engagement with other religious communities, the church shows that its own message of redemption in Christ is relevant to every human context. It is in such 'missionary' activity that the church discovers its own identity, and finds that its own ends are identical with the ends of all.

The church receives its identity from the risen Christ. It receives it day after day, week after week, in the central ritual of Christian belonging – the eucharist. Williams' understanding of the church's sacramental life is located exactly here, as an implication of Christian mission in the world. Henri de Lubac's remark that 'the eucharist makes the church' has become a truism of contemporary theology; but Williams insists that the eucharist loses all meaning if it is ever 'cut off from the pattern of God's mission in the world.'[15] The eucharist is the centre of the church's life only in the sense that it is really 'outside' the church, that it connects us with an energy of life that lies beyond our own resources. In the eucharist, the church celebrates a gift that it never possesses but always receives anew. We receive what we are in order to become what we receive: the body of Christ. Our own identity lies beyond ourselves, so that every act of receiving the eucharist is also a dispossession of whatever identity markers we might have constructed for ourselves. In this way, the eucharist enacts the catholicity of Christ and the elasticity of a community that makes room for the whole world of human experience.

Mission, therefore – the church's public attempt to see its own world as part of the world of others – is in no sense 'external' to the life of the church, any more than the Father's sending of the Son is external to the life of God. Mission is what is most internal to the church's life: it is the church's 'liturgy,' its work of locating itself where Christ is really to be found. As Williams writes in a recent essay:

---

[15] Rowan Williams, 'Imagining the Kingdom: Some Questions for Anglican Worship Today,' in *The Identity of Anglican Worship*, ed. Kenneth Stevenson and Bryan Spinks (Harrisburg, PA: Morehouse, 1991), 10.

God, in speaking to us, 'hides' at the same time in the form of a servant, lest we confuse human power with divine. So in the Body of Christ we have to understand the servant form as essential to the Church's integrity: for it to speak as God speaks . . ., it must also 'hide' its divine origin under the form of poverty and death. Its sacramentality is its capacity to dispossess itself and to be transparent to its root in the divine self-giving.[16]

Every eucharistic celebration is a form of letting go, relinquishing the fantasy that we hold Christ in our possession. For at the table, we find that Christ is already there ahead of us, offering food and drink to 'unworthy but welcome guests.'[17]

To receive the sacrament, then, is to be dislocated and dispossessed. We receive Christ in empty hands; we discover Christ's gift and our own poverty at one and the same moment. That is the meaning of Christian mission: it offers 'both the wealth of a gift and the poverty of those who have first received it.' And this poverty is not a momentary condition that we eventually outgrow; it is part of the continuing experience of a community whose source of life lies beyond itself. Our poverty, our hunger for Christ, 'can only be fully satisfied in a fully reconciled human belonging that does not yet exist in the world.'[18]

The church's mission is to go out looking for Christ in the world, following the risen one on his way across all the self-protective barriers that human beings have erected. As it follows Christ on this path, the church lets go of its own power, privilege, and security. We are 'always likely to forget that Jesus is different from the Church, not the Church's possession'[19]: the eucharist is a tonic against this lethal forgetfulness.

The church, then, exists not for itself but for the sake of a reconciled humanity. We are a laboratory of human possibility, human flourishing, human belonging. And our materials are not test tubes and chemicals, but a book, a chalice, and the broken body of God.

---

[16] Rowan Williams, 'The Church as Sacrament,' *International Journal for the Study of the Christian Church* 10:1 (2010), 8.

[17] Williams, *Mission and Christology*, 20–21.

[18] Williams, *Mission and Christology*, 11.

[19] Williams, *Mission and Christology*, 20.

INTERLUDE

In the Tretyakov Gallery in Moscow stands one of the masterpieces of Russian iconography, the twelfth-century icon of Our Lady of Vladimir (Figure 3). In a poem first drafted in the 1970s, and revised and published in 1994, Williams describes an encounter with the icon:[1]

> Climbs the child, confident,
> up over breast, arm, shoulder;
> while she, alarmed by his bold thrust
> into her face, and the encircling hand,
> looks out imploring fearfully
> and, O, she cries, from her immeasurable eyes,
> O how he clings, see how
> he smothers every pore, like the soft
> shining mistletoe to my black bark,
> she says, I cannot breathe, my eyes
> are aching so.

The Virgin is alarmed by the intensity of the child's affection. He smothers her pores; she cannot breathe, cannot keep him at a safe distance. She looks out at us, imploring us for support against this infant siege, the 'bold thrust' of his terrible hunger and need.

With a poignant touch of realism, the poem hints that the Virgin's eyes are aching from lack of sleep. Like any mother with an infant child, she longs for those coveted intervals of peaceful distance between herself and the child. But with the watchful neediness so characteristic of infants, he climbs over her, pushes his way into her face, and winds an arm possessively around her neck.

---

[1] Rowan Williams, 'Our Lady of Vladimir,' in *The Poems of Rowan Williams* (Grand Rapids: Eerdmans, 2002), 30.

FIGURE 3 Our Lady of Vladimir icon, 12th century. Photo credit: St Isaac of Syria Skete.

Christ's relation to us takes the same form as his relation to the Virgin. Like her, we find ourselves overwhelmed by this demanding infant:

> The child has overlaid us in our beds,
> we cannot close our eyes,
> his weight sits firmly,
> fits over heart and lungs,
> and choked we turn away
> into the window of immeasurable dark
> to shake off the insistent pushing warmth;
> O how he cleaves, no peace
> tonight my lady in your bower,
> you, like us, restless with bruised eyes
> and waking to
> a shining cry on the black bark of sleep.

The child covers us like a heavy blanket. His 'insistent pushing warmth' is too much for us. He cleaves to us just as he clings to his mother, and in a fit of claustrophobia we writhe to be free of him. For us, too, there is 'no peace' from him, no rest for our 'bruised eyes.' We are like sleepless parents, our defences worn down by the exhausting neediness of this child.

Writing elsewhere about the same icon, Williams has described 'the shock of seeing God neither as distant parent nor even as (threatening) adult lover, but as hungry child.'[2] That is what incarnation means: God does not remain at a safe distance, does not leave us be. God is embarrassingly, devastatingly intimate. There is – Williams often returns to this thought – something *frightening* about redemption, something alarming about the relentless intensity of God's love.

The Virgin and child are portrayed again in a poem about a medieval shrine of Our Lady in the little village of Penrhys in Wales.[3] This is an altogether different setting from the august surroundings of the Virgin of Vladimir in Moscow. The Penrhys shrine looks out across the bleak scene of a dilapidated housing development in one of the most disadvantaged parts of Wales:

---

[2] Rowan Williams, *Ponder These Things: Praying with Icons of the Virgin* (Norwich: Canterbury Press, 2002), 38.

[3] Rowan Williams, 'Penrhys,' in *The Poems of Rowan Williams*, 67–68.

The ground falls sharply; into the broken glass,
into the wasted mines, and turds are floating
in the well. Refuse.

May; but the wet, slapping wind is native here,
not fond of holidays. A dour council cleaner,
it lifts discarded

Cartons and condoms and a few stray sheets
of newspaper that the wind sticks
across his face –

The worn sub-Gothic infant, hanging awkwardly
around, glued to a thin mother.
Angelus Novus:

Backing into the granite future, wings spread,
head shaking at the recorded day,
no, he says, refuse,

Not here. Still, the wind drops sharply.
Thin teenage mothers by the bus stop
shake wet hair,

Light cigarettes. One day my bus will come, says one;
they laugh. More use 'n a bloody prince,
says someone else.

It is a dismal scene, grey and windy and wet. The ground is strewn
with garbage, condoms, and broken glass; 'turds are floating' in
the holy well. The earth sinks down towards the old abandoned
mine shafts, while the wind blows sheets of newspaper against
the worn granite shrine. Meanwhile, 'thin teenage mothers' are
hanging around at the bus stop, lighting cigarettes and chatting
idly. We cannot help feeling that a shrine is out of place in this
setting; this, surely, is no place for the holy, no place for Christ and
his mother. But the poem catches us off guard. In fact, the weather-
worn child is also 'hanging awkwardly/around, glued to a thin
mother.' The two of them are quite at home in these inauspicious

surroundings: just another teenage mother and her half-wanted baby. As if a dirty housing estate, more than any cathedral, were the natural habitat of the holy. The poem continues:

The news slips to the ground, the stone dries off,
smoke and steam drift uphill
and tentatively

Finger the leisure centre's tense walls and stairs.
The babies cry under the sun,
they and the thin girls

Comparing notes, silently, on shared
unwritten stories of the bloody stubbornness
of getting someone born.

As the rain stops and the babies begin to cry, there is a moment of silent identification between the Virgin and the teenage girls. These unpromising mothers – Mary and the rest – wait idly together, 'comparing notes' on the visceral hardships of childbirth and motherhood.

The poem's pathos comes from its patient observation of the scene, the realism that refuses to flinch from the ordinary and the profane. It is like the long single-take scene in Tarkovsky's 1979 film *Stalker*, where the camera slowly pans across an endless trail of debris, observing each thing with a disquieting, undiscriminating attentiveness. It is in a scene like this that we can, for once, glimpse the meaning of the incarnation. A teenage mother smoking cigarettes at a dirty bus stop, her life still reeling from 'the bloody stubbornness of getting someone born' – that is what incarnation looks like. Christ is defamiliarized when we perceive him like this, with a grittiness untouched by religious disinfectant. At the same time, the bleak tenderness with which the poem observes the young mothers invests them with a sort of nimbus of dignity. They are, in an oblique way, taken into Mary's confidence. It is with *them* (not with the reader) that she compares notes. As though these girls, with their cheap lipstick, their strollers and their cigarettes, come closest to comprehending the hard unsentimental miracle of the incarnation of God.

8

Saints

fingers closing
like a child's on the found flesh.
My joy. My joy.[1]

St Francis of Assisi wore the word 'fool' like 'a feather in his cap':
so G. K. Chesterton observed in his memorable biography of that
eccentric saintly life. 'He had made a fool of himself,' Chesterton
writes. 'There was not a rag of him left that was not ridiculous.'[2]

We learn the most about language by studying its extreme forms
– especially the language of poetry. What poetry is to the millennia-
long experiment of language, so the saints are to that vast, untidy
workshop, the laboratory of humanity. We learn most about human
beings not from pale mediocre cases, but from an aberration, the
strange and unnerving spectacle of a holy life.

If you ask Roman Catholic believers what it is that makes
the church distinctive, they will probably begin speaking of the
sacramental hierarchy by which the whole church is ordered and
held together. Put the same question to contemporary Protestant
theologians, and they will start telling you about 'practices,' those
communal behaviours by which the church marks itself out as an
alternative social order. But if you ask a Russian Orthodox believer
what makes the church distinctive, she will think at once of holy
lives: when she says the word 'church,' it is not the face of the
bishop that comes to mind, nor merely her own face, but the faces
of the saints.

---

[1] Rowan Williams, 'Sarov, August 2003: The Outer Hermitage,' in *Headwaters*
(Oxford: Perpetua, 2008), 17.

[2] G. K. Chesterton, *St Francis of Assisi*, in *The Collected Works of G. K. Chesterton* II
(San Francisco: Ignatius, 1986), 71–72.

Why are the walls of Russian churches so crowded and cluttered with icons of the saints? It is not because the Orthodox love pictures, but because they love *light*. For the icons are not art works, but windows: they are the small openings through which the light of God bursts in upon the gathered church. It is here, in the lives and prayers of the saints, that the church is irradiated and sustained. The saints have lived in such proximity to God that they become a kind of intercession for the rest of us. God looks at us through them: they are God's windows.

The great figures of modern Russian theology were often deeply sceptical about the importance of hierarchy, clericalism, and ecclesiastical order. Williams admiringly notes that Sergius Bulgakov 'has next to nothing to say about the role of hierarchy,' and that the pages he devotes to ordained ministry 'have about them a very slightly dutiful character.'[3] In the west, anti-clericalism is usually viewed as an attack on the very heart of the church; but the Orthodox think that the church's heart lies elsewhere, not in officially normative patterns but in those particular lives that have drawn most deeply from the real wellspring of life.

In the preceding chapters, I have explored the development of Williams' theology of the church; but running through his ecclesial vision, like a red thread, is a theology of sanctity. And it is here that all his thinking about the church is really held together. For him, the saints occupy the same normative position that hierarchy occupies in Catholic ecclesiology or that practice occupies in much contemporary theology. That is why his writing on church order, authority, and ritual is typically critical instead of affirmative; his attitude towards ecclesial power and position is summed up in the pithy observation that holding office in the church is bad for the soul: 'Think of what Coca-Cola does to your teeth.'[4] Like the Orthodox, Williams sees the church not primarily in terms of form or ritual, but in terms of its saints. And when he refers to the 'saints', it is not a generic term for the whole company of believers: he is thinking of particular holy lives, of sanctity as one distinct way of being human.

But isn't there a danger here of cultivating merely another form of spiritual elitism – replacing the clerics with the saints? Pierre

---

[3] Rowan Williams, *A Margin of Silence: The Holy Spirit in Russian Orthodox Theology* (Québec: Éditions du Lys Vert, 2008), 33.

[4] From his response to Bishop Spong in *Church Times* 17 July 1998.

Pascal's study of Russian piety, which Williams translated into English in 1976, notes that, for the Orthodox, the saints are not rare figures; you may find them in any neighbourhood or village. Moreover, 'the Russians do not see such a gulf existing between layman and priest, secular and monk, sinner and saint, and so do not regard these people as beings apart, to be admired from a distance.'[5] The saint doesn't stand at a distance from ordinary human experience but is more deeply involved in it, since the saint stands closer to the source of what it means to be a full human being.

Williams' understanding of the church thus has two main poles: the slow, limping growth of ordinary believers on the one hand and the startling presence of holy lives on the other. There is a tension here, but no contradiction. Sinners and saints belong together – like a house and a home. Saints, as the word suggests, have a sanctifying influence on the whole church; they belong to the church's atmosphere, its spiritual milieu. Holy lives sustain the Christian community on its tortuous pilgrimage towards maturity. To put it rather baldly, saints show that sanctity is possible; they prove that it is possible to live before God and to live before others in light of God. The fact that there are saints teaches us to be patient: patient with the more vulnerable members of the church, patient with those whose growth seems halting and uncertain – patient, perhaps, even with ourselves.

For Williams, the saints embody something of Christ's kenosis: making themselves nothing, they make room for God. But this yielding of the self to God does not mean a sheer 'immersion' of the saint in the Other, as Williams says in criticism of the Jewish philosopher Edith Wyschogrod.[6] Holiness is not the self's erasure, but its intensification. Williams is fond of the analogy of a musician's performance: the musician becomes more gloriously herself as she allows her own ego to become completely transparent to the mind and intention of the composer. The performer's kenosis is not emptiness but true fullness, a 'saturation' in which one self lovingly yields to another. In this act of willed displacement, the self becomes

---

[5] Pierre Pascal, *The Religion of the Russian People*, trans. Rowan Williams (Crestwood, NY: St Vladimir's Seminary Press, 1976), 49.

[6] Rowan Williams, review of Edith Wyschogrod, *Saints and Postmodernism*, in *Modern Theology* 8 (1992), 305–7.

more acute, more distinctive, yet also more expansive and elastic and capable of giving.[7]

Again, the saint's self-displacement has nothing to do with mere temperamental meekness, or what ecclesiastical leaders like to call 'humility.' We need only think of a clergyman like Mr Collins in Jane Austen's *Pride and Prejudice* to recall that the most servile humility and the most wildly delusional vanity go hand in hand. Preoccupation with my own humility is just vanity by another name. Saints are not those who cultivate their own self-abnegation; they are engaged in the honest and forgetful business of giving themselves freely and freely receiving from others. In a remark on the dangers of religious humility, Williams observes that the kenosis of Christian sociality means not that we should go about saying 'no' to who we really are, but that 'each self hears its "yes" from the other and not from its own depths.'[8] Indeed a saintly life might be marked by a sort of 'holy egotism,' a term he has used of figures like Desmond Tutu and Karl Barth. Such egotism is neither pride nor false humility, only an unselfconscious enjoyment of the expansive capacities of the self. The ego is displaced just by regarding it lightly, by treating it with reckless enjoyment, as though it were a gift. C. S. Lewis has finely observed that humility means enjoying your own gifts as though they were somebody else's; you could design the world's best cathedral and rejoice just as much as if someone else had done it.[9] This means perceiving yourself as a gift, and so remaining free enough to go on sharing gladly, unselfconsciously, and indiscriminately.

That is what Williams means by holy egotism: not pushing everybody else to the edges to make room for your own inflated ego, but sharing yourself around in a way that helps others to become more truly themselves. Not Jane Austen's craven clergyman, then, but someone like the title character of the 1987 film, *Babette's Feast* (a film that Williams has described as an 'animated icon').[10]

---

[7] Rowan Williams, *Tokens of Trust: An Introduction to Christian Belief* (Louisville: WJK, 2007), 74.

[8] Williams, *Margin of Silence*, 31.

[9] C. S. Lewis, *The Screwtape Letters* (London: Geoffrey Bles, 1942), Chapter 14.

[10] In the 2004 debate with Philip Pullman: 'The Dark Materials Debate: Life, God, the Universe,' *The Telegraph*, 17 March 2004.

When unassuming Babette wins the lottery, she spends the entire fortune on the flagrant extravagance of one glorious, stupendous dinner for her friends. That is what the holy life looks like: a joyous intensification, a generous and reckless enlargement of the self, as one particular human life is placed wholly at the disposal of others.

So the amplification of the self is at the same time its displacement: the self becomes freer and more expansive only when it ceases to see itself as the centre of things. The ego is both enlarged and deposed. The result is that curious, eccentric figure in Christian tradition, a figure celebrated by hagiographers and lovingly delineated by novelists like Dostoevsky, Graham Greene, and Shusaku Endo – the 'holy fool,' or what the Russian church affectionately calls the *yurodivy*. This is the figure that looms so large in Williams' thought. His personal and intellectual world is peopled by zany characters, intellectual misfits, spiritual neurotics – Wittgenstein and Donald MacKinnon, Gillian Rose and Simone Weil, the Carmelites and the desert fathers. Williams' whole imaginative life is shaped by such characters; and we shall never understand what he means by words like 'God' or 'church' or 'spirituality' until we observe this tender preoccupation with the figure of the holy fool.

Saints are not typically balanced, well-rounded people. They do not necessarily possess exemplary virtues or a notable degree of psychological integration. They are, Williams says, typically 'pretty uneven, not to say confused characters,' whose lives have been 'knocked off balance' by the strange world of God.[11] That is why we ourselves are knocked off balance when we encounter a holy life: we reel in the presence of sanctity, just as we might reel before the strangely distorted lines of perspective in a Russian icon. The perspective of the saint's life seems skewed – but only because it is really *our* world that is bent out of shape. In the weirdness of the saint, we are glimpsing the geometry of another world.

Thus we are often incapable of recognizing holiness when we see it. Saints are frequently despised or condemned during their lifetimes and only later recognized – often rather grudgingly – by ecclesiastical authority. In a sermon on the life of a nineteenth-century priest, Marie-Joseph Huvelin, Williams describes him as

---

[11] Rowan Williams, 'Saints,' in Joan Chittister and Rowan Williams, *Uncommon Gratitude: Alleluia for All That Is* (Collegeville, MN: Liturgical Press, 2010), 71–73.

psychologically damaged, 'a deeply injured and fearful man.' Can we discern the sanctity of a life like this, a broken and in some respects failed human story?

> Can we, with our rhetoric of the identity of holiness and wholeness, begin to cope with the 'sanctity' of a man whose mental and emotional balance was so limited? A man less than perfectly sane? We do not here have to do with the question of the *holy fool* but the question – harder for our day – of the holy neurotic.[12]

When we speak of sanctity, Williams thinks, we are not talking about 'wholeness,' but almost its opposite. George Herbert compared the preacher to a panel of stained glass in an English chapel: by itself the glass is dim and fragmented, but by daylight it is resplendent.[13] In the same way, saints may be damaged and unmended, but through the 'brittle crazy glass' of their lives, the whole church is startlingly transfigured, washed in the light and colour of the bright shining world of God.

The uniqueness of saints, then, is not that they are uniquely whole but simply that they are really 'awake,' acutely aware of 'the glorious and troubling difference of God.'[14] In his study of Teresa of Avila, Williams writes in a similar vein of the distinctiveness of those whom the church calls 'mystics.' Mystics do not necessarily enjoy spectacular experiences of the divine; they are simply lives that have been shot through by some of the radiance of the Christian story – even if those lives remain broken and brittle, an ambiguous rather than a clear witness to grace.[15]

Indeed, Williams often suggests that God's real work in the church is typically hidden and ambiguous. Those who seem central to the church's institutional life may in fact play no part in God's activity; the real work is happening somewhere else. The risen Christ is quietly and powerfully at work in the formation of holy lives, even when those lives are quite marginal to the visible activity

---

[12] Rowan Williams, 'The Abbé Huvelin,' in *A Ray of Darkness: Sermons and Reflections* (Cambridge, MA: Cowley, 1994), 181.

[13] George Herbert, 'The Windows,' in *The English Poems of George Herbert*, ed. Helen Wilcox (Cambridge: Cambridge University Press, 2007).

[14] Williams, 'Saints,' 74–75.

[15] Rowan Williams, *Teresa of Avila* (London: Continuum, 1991).

of the church. We might call this an ecclesiology of the margins: those at the social edges are in fact at the real centre of God's work. In the Gospel of Mark, it is finally only a Roman soldier who recognizes Jesus and confesses the secret of his identity (Mk 15.39); the outsider discerns what the inner circle fails to grasp.

In this vision of the church, two powerful streams merge in Williams' thought, the austere social particularism of Welsh Nonconformity and the capacious catholicity of Russian ecclesiology. The Russian tradition buoys up his invincible confidence that there will always be holy lives to empower and irradiate the church, to keep the church in contact with the life of Christ; the Welsh stream is manifest in a lingering scepticism about ecclesial power and the sort of self-assured clericalism that Donald MacKinnon fiercely denounced as 'ecclesiological fundamentalism.'[16] Even in the presence of his own community Christ remains a stranger, subverting the wise and the powerful, filling the hungry with good things but sending the rich away empty.

Williams thus speaks of God's 'cavalier way' with our own structures, boundaries, and expectations. God cannot be relied upon to work through the appropriate channels; there is something anarchic and unprincipled about God's activity:

> What if the life that fuels the Church through prayer is not the routine prayer of the worshipping community, not even the prayer of the religious orders, but moments of exposure and insight, or of desperately needy openness to God on the part of very irregular Christians? Isn't this actually what Jesus' story of the Pharisee and the tax-collector might suggest? What if the Church really lives from the prayer and experience of those it least values in its public talk?[17]

This is what Williams calls 'the hiddenness of Christ in the Church.' It means that there is never a direct identity between ecclesial practices and divine action; and it also means that the church does not need to be anxious about protecting itself or securing its future,

---

[16] Donald MacKinnon, 'Kenosis and Establishment,' in *The Stripping of the Altars* (London: Collins, 1969).

[17] The quotations that follow are from Rowan Williams, *Ponder These Things: Praying with Icons of the Virgin* (Norwich: Canterbury Press, 2002), 48–54.

nor 'constantly . . . reassuring itself of its success.' Indeed, if Christ's
work is hidden, it may really be our successes that stand most in the
way. We need only recall the story of the rich young man to see that
it is often our successes more than our failures that keep us far from
the kingdom (Mk 10.17–31).

In the same way, Williams thinks that it is often our failures that
bring us closest to the well of life. It is often only in failure that
the ego is dethroned and decentred: at last we are drawn out of
ourselves, set free to locate the real source of our being in Christ.
His power is made perfect in weakness. 'Those parts of our own
individual experience that seem least pious or "together",' Williams
says, 'may be the points at which we are exposed to God, and so the
points from which we most truly come to live in Christ.' It is here, in
the most vulnerable and difficult dimensions of our experience, that
God's kenotic omnipotence is most deeply and secretly at work.

Williams has even suggested that the lives of the saints might
be the only legitimate apologetics, the only persuasive argument
for the existence of God. Much of what we call 'God' is fantasy,
a self-protective projection of our own wishes and anxieties. But
the anguish with which these 'holy neurotics' stand before God,
the traumatic reshaping of their identities, the appalling purgation
of their loves and desires – all this shows that their God could not
possibly be just another instance of Freudian wish fulfilment. 'If
they take God that seriously, at least this isn't some cosy made-up
way of making yourself feel better.'[18]

Saints don't necessarily provide any easy spiritual consolation.
But they do something more important: they let God in. That is
the best way to demonstrate God's existence. Our religiosity often
conspires to make God quite incredible, a God accessible only to
the insiders or the elite. But the saint, Williams writes, makes God
credible and available; the saint 'takes responsibility for God's
believability.'[19] In a world of darkness, the saint throws open the
windows and lets God in.

In a profound meditation on iconography, Pavel Florensky
ventures a single-sentence apologetics of the Christian faith: 'There
exists the icon of the Holy Trinity by St Andrei Rublev; therefore

---

[18] Williams, *Tokens of Trust*, 21.
[19] Williams, *Tokens of Trust*, 23.

God exists.'[20] This startling remark might be taken as a gloss on Williams' theology of saints. The saint is an argument for the existence of God. As icons are painted on gold, so the stories of saints are written on a background of light. That is why they are often so strange, eccentric, confused, and neurotic. Their lives are completely unintelligible, defying all explanation – *unless* the explanation is God.

And so we arrive at last at the Christian doctrine of God. How does Rowan Williams think about God? God is the grammar of holy lives, their dark and dazzling intelligibility.

---

[20] Pavel Florensky, *Iconostasis*, trans. Donald Sheehan and Olga Andrejev (Crestwood, NY: St Vladimir's Seminary Press, 1996), 68.

9

Desire

But we shall sit and speak around
one table, share one food, one earth.[1]

Since becoming Archbishop of Canterbury in 2002, Williams has devoted much of his scholarly attention to the Christian doctrine of God, publishing a stream of essays on the work of Augustine, as well as on classical figures like Thomas Aquinas and John of the Cross. While his early intellectual energy was devoted to considerations of sociality, language, and meaning, this process of questioning has culminated in a searching re-evaluation of the doctrine of the trinity, interpreted as an account of the intelligibility of human desire, meaning, and belonging. Marx thought that the grammar of society, its deepest underlying logic, was economics; Freud thought it was instinct; Williams argues that the real grammar of social life is a wellspring of love and life – the holy trinity.

Williams' thought on the trinity is nourished at every point by the work of Augustine. All the intricacies of his mature theology of the trinity can be traced to a conception of desire which he first articulated in a 1986 essay on Augustine.[2] In this study, he takes up Augustine's famous distinction between 'use' and 'enjoyment': to 'enjoy' (*frui*) something is to choose it for its own sake alone, while to 'use' (*uti*) something is to choose it for the sake of a higher goal. Thus Augustine argues that God alone can be 'enjoyed' as the ultimate goal of our love, whereas finite objects of love should be 'used' to direct us beyond themselves to the love of God. To enjoy

---

[1] Rowan Williams, 'Rublev,' in *The Poems of Rowan Williams* (Grand Rapids: Eerdmans, 2002), 51.

[2] Rowan Williams, 'Language, Reality and Desire in Augustine's *De Doctrina*,' *Journal of Literature and Theology* 3:2 (1989); first presented at a conference in 1986.

something is to 'make it the end and sum of your joy.'[3] Williams
finds here the basis for a Christian doctrine of desire. Our greatest
temptation is to try to possess things, to treat the world as something
that could be enjoyed as an end in itself. But this means we are
really viewing the world as existing for *our* sake: as though the
world were defined by its capacity to satisfy our own desires. We
might imagine that we are valuing the world more highly when we
treat it as an end in itself, but, Williams argues, the reverse is really
the case. If our desire terminates in any finite object, then we have
consumed that object, allowing its meaning to be exhausted by our
desire. Paradoxically, only the 'use' of worldly things enables them
to remain separate from us, inexhaustibly themselves, expanding
our love as they deflect it towards an infinite object of love. Only a
love directed towards God can rescue the world from the egotistical
possessiveness of human desire. Williams argues, therefore, for 'a
language which indefinitely postpones fulfilment or enjoyment.' All
worldly loves are marked by 'non-finality, growing, and learning';
to seek the finality of satisfied desire within the created order is to
rob the world of its objectivity (its capacity to be *more* than what
we desire), and to cut ourselves off from the process of growth in
love. Any cessation of desire is illegitimate.

This Augustinian theology of desire was developed further in
Williams' controversial lecture on 'The Body's Grace,' delivered to
the Lesbian and Gay Christian Movement in London in 1989.[4] Here
he argues that the church's traditional teaching on homosexuality
arises from a faulty view of desire. The church has often been quick
to sanction heterosexual marriage in terms of its instrumental
usefulness. It is a means of gratification – a 'remedy against sin,'
as the Book of Common Prayer has it – and a way of achieving
the goal of reproduction. This attitude, however, evades the whole
question of what human desire means. Echoing his 1986 analysis
of Augustine, Williams argues that desire cannot simply terminate
in its object; we cannot love for the sake of some definite 'payoff,'
since this would be to possess the object of love as though it existed
only for our sake. In sexual relations, we are not 'instruments
for each other's gratification.' Indeed, Williams defines sexual

---

[3] Augustine, *De doctrina christiana*, 1.33.

[4] Rowan Williams, *The Body's Grace: The 10th Michael Harding Memorial Address* (London: Lesbian and Gay Christian Movement, 1989).

perversion as 'refusing the otherness of the material world' by bringing it under our own control. Perversion occurs wherever desire is 'asymmetrical,' wherever another person's body becomes a mere device of gratification instead of a separate and objective source of desire. Thus Williams wryly remarks: 'If this suggests that, in a great many cultural settings, the socially licensed norm of heterosexual intercourse is a "perversion" – well, that is a perfectly serious suggestion.' In contrast, healthy sexual love is that in which each partner 'waits upon the desire of the other.' My body becomes the cause of joy only as it is given over to the joy of another person: 'to desire my joy is to desire the joy of the one I desire.' The meaning of sexual desire, therefore, becomes vividly clear in the case of the 'non-functional joy' of homosexual desire. Indeed Williams comes close to presenting same-sex desire as the paradigmatic form of human love. 'Same-sex love annoyingly poses the question of what the meaning of desire is in itself, not considered as instrumental to some other process': it is a window in which we can more readily glimpse the meaning of human desire as such.

In the 1980s, then, Williams' thinking about same-sex desire and his thinking about the trinity are intertwined. His apologia for same-sex desire is bound up with the very centre of a Christian under-standing of God: that is the whole significance of the 1989 lecture, and it is why the lecture was (rightly) perceived as a fundamental challenge to the church's thinking on sexuality. Williams himself insists that a theology of human sexuality is not 'a marginal eccentricity in the doctrinal spectrum,' but a truth deeply embedded in Christian belief in God as trinity. By the time he had delivered this 1989 lecture, Williams' conception of desire was in place, and he had laid the foundation for a systematic reformulation of the doctrine of the trinity. That reformulation has been his most important scholarly contribution throughout his years as Archbishop of Canterbury.

Following Augustine, Williams understands God as an infinite ground of objectivity, truthfulness, and love. God loves, and this love is so attentive, so objective, that within God there opens up a differentiation: God loves God. Yet in this twofold movement of love, neither partner can simply terminate its desire in the other. Any desire that is gratified would be 'abortive,' a failure of love.[5]

---

[5] Rowan Williams, 'What Does Love Know? St Thomas on the Trinity,' *New Blackfriars* 82:964 (2001), 272.

So the Father and the Son have an excess of desire for one another; each loves the other objectively with a desire that is never gratified. The surplus of desire is 'deflected' into a holy Third: the Spirit. It is the Spirit who, as it were, rescues God from a narcissistic collapse into mere twoness, mere mutual gratification of desire. The Spirit sustains the exchange of love between Father and Son precisely by being *more* than that exchange, by personifying their mutual excess of love. It is the Spirit who takes the love of the Father and Son and constantly draws it outwards into an ever widening circle.[6] The Spirit – to echo the language of Gillian Rose – is the 'agon' of love, the work by which the distance between Father and Son is sustained.

In turn, the Son loves not only the love bestowed on him by the Father but also its excess. The Son loves what the Father loves, which is that there is 'more' than the Father's love for the Son. Thus, what the Son really loves is the absence of satisfied desire. God loves the very negativity of love – or as Augustine argues, what love loves is *loving*. In short, God is a trinity of love: the lover, the beloved, and a constantly expanding surplus of love itself. God's love never comes to rest but forms a widening field as it surges back and forth, infinite giving, infinite receiving, infinite deflection of desire.

This is a dauntingly complex account of the trinity, to be sure. The picture comes into focus when we consider Williams' interpretation of the work of Sergius Bulgakov.[7] For Bulgakov the trinity is a kenotic reality, in which the Father empties the divine being into the Son, holding nothing back. Bulgakov describes this as an act of 'self-devastation': in begetting the Son, the Father 'lays himself waste' in order to give his whole being to the Son, and likewise the Son divests himself of any individual status and wills to have his being wholly from the Father. So how do the Father and Son maintain their distinctiveness, when each is dispossessed, handing everything over to the other? The answer, for Bulgakov, is the Holy Spirit. As Williams puts it, 'the potential tragedy of mutual

---

[6] Rowan Williams, 'The Deflections of Desire: Negative Theology in Trinitarian Disclosure,' in *Silence and the Word: Negative Theology and Incarnation*, ed. Oliver Davies and Denys Turner (Cambridge: Cambridge University Press, 2002).

[7] Rowan Williams, *A Margin of Silence: The Holy Spirit in Russian Orthodox Theology* (Québec: Éditions du Lys Vert, 2008), 22–24.

annihilation is overcome in the joy of the Spirit.' It is as though the identity of the Father might have collapsed into that of the Son; but the Spirit comes between them, securing their objectivity by holding them apart. The Spirit thus brings the Father and the Son into mutual articulacy, 'into vision' before one another, sustaining their love by sustaining the distance that love requires.

FIGURE 4   Andrei Rublev, icon of the Holy Trinity, c. 1410. Photo credit: St Isaac of Syria Skete.

Williams' emphasis on the deflection of desire is influenced not only by traditional Christian texts but also by a piece of visual theology which has been an important part of his spiritual life over many years: Rublev's icon of the trinity (Figure 4). In Rublev's image – the only picture of God that looks as if it were drawn from life, as Williams once remarked – each of the three figures draws our gaze, but then deflects our eye towards the next figure at the table, until we have circled back to where we started. The vacant seat is for us: to take a seat at the table is to enter into the same movement of life and love in which the three figures are caught up. Communion with God is self-displacement. We discover that our identity is really located not within ourselves but in this pattern of love and deflection. We now perceive ourselves as the 'site' of God's own self-displacement and self-bestowal.[8] We recognize ourselves, in a word, as *loved*.

Thus the life of God does not erase the distinctiveness of the self – it is not what Simone Weil calls the ecstatic 'decreation' of the self. Rather, Williams sees this rhythm of self-displacement as yielding a heightened realization of identity and particularity. Recall the analogy of musical performance: the composer's intentions are realized through the performer, on account of a momentary landslide of the ego. Yet the subjectivity of the performer is never more acute; human beings become most fully themselves when they locate the centre of the ego outside itself, in another personal source. That is how Williams interprets Augustine's insight that knowing the self and knowing God are inseparable. Paradoxically, 'the movement into our createdness' is simultaneously 'a movement into God's own life as turned outwards.'[9]

Knowledge of the self comes through the willed displacement of the self to God. While Williams thinks of the trinitarian life as a movement of kenosis and reciprocity, he is thus quite reserved about much contemporary talk of divine 'relationality,' or the mythological image of a 'social trinity.' Theologians like Jürgen Moltmann have drawn attention to the relational shape of divine life, but in rejecting the picture of God as a single subject they fall into the equally crude representation of God as *three* such subjects. In contrast, Williams

---

[8] Williams, 'Deflections of Desire,' 129.

[9] Rowan Williams, 'Sapientia and the Trinity: Reflections on the *De Trinitate*,' in *Collectanea Augustiniana*, ed. Bernard Bruning et al. (Louvain: Leuven University Press, 1990), 321.

argues that an Augustinian account of the trinity 'demythologizes' the autonomous subject by locating human selfhood within the movement of divine self-giving.[10] The contemporary notion of a 'social trinity' allows the Cartesian subject to remain unchallenged, and even to be projected back into the life of God. In Williams' view, the trinity is neither a single sovereign subject (Barth) nor several egalitarian subjects (Moltmann), but an energy of self-divesting love which explodes the whole idea of autonomous subjectivity.

There is a darker side here too. As we move into the divine life, our selfish desires are purged and redirected. God never satisfies our desire but constantly deflects it, so that we are drawn into a love without limit or closure. For human beings – caught in the feverish grip of self-centredness – this infinite refusal of gratification can only be felt as 'pain and privation,' even though it is true freedom. We inevitably experience God's love not as fulfilment but as 'darkness and absence.' Even Jesus, as a human subject, experiences this privation in the agony of Gethsemane and Golgotha. The cross is the annihilation of his desire, since it is the annihilation of any *God* who would merely satisfy human yearning. But it is at just this point, in the stripping bare of Jesus' desire, that God is most active and most free. Jesus' whole self has given way to the will of God, so that God no longer stands over against Jesus as 'a determinate other.'[11] At the core of his relation to God, therefore, is the dark night of the soul – the darkness of love.

Love grants what we desire only by surpassing our desire. Love eludes gratification and lures us on, producing a widening spiral of desire. That is what it means to say that we 'love' God. Not that God gratifies us by fulfilling our fantasies, but that we have abandoned ourselves to the great landslide of self-displacement that is going on forever between the Father, the Son, and the Holy Spirit. If desire is deflected within God, then God is infinitely desirable, a reality we can encounter only in self-abandonment.

For Williams, then, the doctrine of the trinity is about *grace*. It is an articulation of the grammar of 'divine gratuity and other-centredness.'[12] Or, more succinctly, it is simply the gospel. It means that God's relation to us is wholly bound up with God's relation

---

[10] Williams, 'Sapientia and the Trinity,' 331.

[11] Williams, 'Deflections of Desire,' 120–26.

[12] Williams, 'What Does Love Know,' 270.

to God. The community of believers participates in Christ's filial relation to the Father. As we are aligned with Christ, we become 'the multiple echo of the Word's response to the Father.'[13] Thus, as Williams says of Augustine, the doctrine of the trinity is really 'nothing other than a teasing out of what it is to be converted and to come to live in Christ'[14] – a picture of what human lives look like when they are located in the love of God. The image of God in humanity, likewise, is not 'the mind' but 'the mind of the saint.'[15] The triune life is reflected in those human lives that have become (literally) eccentric, located beyond themselves in the divine giving.

So at the bottom of everything is love. That is all Williams really means to say in those painstaking meditations on the trinity to which he has devoted so much scholarly energy in recent years. Love is reality, love is clarity, love is truth – and it is possible to go on trusting in that love even when our experience is marked by failure and tragedy. As Williams had already intimated in his 1989 lecture on sexual desire:

> The whole story of creation, incarnation and our incorporation into Christ's body tells us that God desires us *as if we were God*, as if we were that unconditional response to God's giving that [God] makes in the life of the Trinity. We are created so that we may be caught up in this, so that we may grow into the whole-hearted love of God by learning that God loves us as God loves God. The life of the Christian community has as its rationale . . . the task of teaching us this: so ordering our relations that human beings may see themselves as desired, as the occasion of joy.[16]

The holy trinity is an infinite well of objectivity, truthfulness, and love. The threefold surge of God's love floods our desires and sweeps away our selfish fantasies. The doctrine of the trinity is the criticism of desire. As a human community is drawn into this pattern of threefold energy, we are aligned with the shape of divine

---

[13] Rowan Williams, 'Augustine and the Psalms,' *Interpretation* 58:1 (2004), 21.

[14] Rowan Williams, '*De Trinitate*,' in *Augustine through the Ages: An Encyclopedia*, ed. Allan D. Fitzgerald (Grand Rapids: Eerdmans, 1999), 850.

[15] Rowan Williams, 'The Paradoxes of Self-Knowledge in the *De Trinitate*,' in *Collectanea Augustiniana* (New York: Peter Lang, 1993), 131.

[16] Williams, *The Body's Grace*, 3.

reality. We are aligned with love, and we begin to body forth that love in our relations with one another, freely laying ourselves waste for one another, and freely receiving everything back again. By living in the environment of the trinity, in the milieu of the Spirit, we begin, in spite of ourselves, to live in love. And the mark of a community of love is growth, an ever-expanding capacity for generosity, commitment, and truth.

In all this Williams proves himself to be, as he once said of Hans Urs von Balthasar, 'one of those eccentrics who assume that the whole breadth of human reality can be illuminated by the Nicene and Chalcedonian faith.'[17] The questions he has been puzzling over for so long – questions of truth, trust, meaning, and sociality – are finally resolved here, in contemplation of the mystery of a God whose life is love, of three persons seated around a table, silently beckoning us to take up the empty seat.

---

[17] Rowan Williams, 'Balthasar and Difference' [1998], in *Wrestling with Angels*, ed. Mike Higton (Grand Rapids: Eerdmans, 2007), 85.

10

Hope

Stand up, come in and sing us out of doors.[1]

Williams' theology of the trinity is, then, a vision of negativity, incompletion, and unconsummated desire. Like Noah's dove going forth across the face of the earth but finding no place to rest, so God's love unceasingly goes forth and returns, never alighting. God is not only what we hope for but also the frustration of our hopes and desires. 'God is what we have not yet understood, the sign of a strange and unpredictable future.'[2] The negativity of divine love opens into a negative eschatology. Christian hope, Williams argues, cannot neutralize the tragic dimensions of human experience, nor posit any 'total perspective' that would supply a definitive account of the meaning of history.

Religious eschatology is, typically, a projection of human wishes on to the blank screen of the future. In contrast, Williams reinterprets eschatology as a criticism of human desire. The result is a non-teleological eschatology, reflecting the austere vision of T. S. Eliot's *Four Quartets*. Here the fundamental imperative is to remain patient:

> Wait without hope
> For hope would be hope for the wrong thing.

Like Eliot, Williams is uncomfortable with hope because of its tendency towards fantasy and projection. We have succumbed to a

---

[1] Rowan Williams, 'Crossings,' in *The Poems of Rowan Williams* (Grand Rapids: Eerdmans, 2002), 36.

[2] Rowan Williams, *The Wound of Knowledge* [1979] (2nd ed.; London: Darton, Longman & Todd, 1990), 66.

profound spiritual dementia, and we no longer remember what to hope for; even when we do hope, it is for all the wrong things. Christian talk about the age to come tends dangerously towards such fantasy. How many of our ultimate hopes can really be reduced to longings for personal gratification, personal vindication, or catastrophic judgment on our enemies? Our hopes and disappointments are centred on ourselves, instead of on the formation of a new human community, the 'new creation' of the gospel (2 Cor. 5.17).

Theologians writing about eschatology often give the impression of a sort of cosmic optimism: history might have its dark subplots but there is a great dénouement coming in the last chapter, which will situate everything in a new light. Here the structure of history is rather like that of a Victorian novel: the whole story, with its intricate web of unhappy subplots, achieves a sudden, triumphant resolution at the end. There are no loose ends, no irrational remainders. That is what eschatology is often taken to mean: a clever trick in the last chapter, a scenario 'in which . . . everything concludes to the satisfaction of everybody' (to quote the final chapter heading of Dickens' *Pickwick Papers*).

But Williams insists that God's redemptive activity does not cancel out the experience of tragedy. Nor does God achieve a final theodicy that balances the books, as though a quantitative measure of ultimate good could outweigh even one experience of human tragedy. Again, for Williams eschatology is not the end of the historical sequence, not the hidden *telos* of the world. That would not be the transfiguration of tragedy, but only its denial. As the New Testament makes clear, Christian hope is most pronounced where history is experienced as a spiritual catastrophe. Christian hope does not invalidate this tragic vision, but reaffirms it – just as Christ's resurrection does not cancel out the crucifixion, but transfigures it and discloses its inner significance.

This means the end has only a negative relation to our speech and our lives: it is that which we cannot posit. We refuse to align ourselves with an imagined end, a conclusion that could validate and vindicate our stories. Christian hope can too easily descend into a theory of who will win; no misunderstanding is more poisonous than to imagine Christ as the one who secures our place as history's victors. Christ's exaltation is a cross. He rules history not by seizing control but by entering into our world and gently transforming it from within.

In one of his earliest published essays, a 1974 study of Russian Orthodox conceptions of the Holy Spirit,[3] Williams already developed this tragic interpretation of Christian hope. The age to come is not a new temporal period following on the heels of the present one, otherwise eschatology would denote just another part of the historical sequence, instead of something altogether new. Further, Christian hope has a tragic dimension, since it is a hope for the transformation of real embodied human relationships. The Spirit does not overcome the fragmentation and difficulty of social life, but draws us more deeply into that awkward and costly unity of human community. Our lives together are undergoing repair, and this, for Williams, *is* redemption. The difficulty of sociality is not a temporary obstacle to be overcome, then, not even eschatologically. Christian hope is directed towards the transfiguration of the full range of our human experience in this world: 'The communion of the Spirit is a communion in horror and glory.' Williams draws on Paul Evdokimov's claim that the Spirit is the beginning of the parousia in our history – though, characteristically, he demythologizes this Russian theme by relating it to new beginnings within the ordinary fabric of human relationships.

Though Williams retains the language of hope, then, what he really commends is a sort of patience beyond hope, a suspension of our own desires before the unpredictable newness of God. God is 'both our frustration and our hope.'[4] This is eschatology not as a description of 'last things,' but as a moral vision that disciplines our desires and fixes our attention on God. Paradoxical as it might sound, Williams believes eschatological language is legitimate only to the extent that it refuses to posit any theory of the end. As Jesus evokes God by telling worldly stories that do not even mention God, so Christians point to the life of the world to come by holding ourselves open to the future without projecting any of our own wishes on to it. This is a sort of imaginative asceticism, a cancellation of traditional eschatological imagery, so that the language of hope is translated into the register of moral attention.

---

[3] Rowan Williams, 'The Spirit of the Age to Come,' *Sobornost* 6:9 (1974), 613–26.

[4] Rowan Williams, 'The Health of the Spirit,' in *Public Life and the Place of the Church: Reflections to Honour the Bishop of Oxford*, ed. Michael Brierley (Aldershot: Ashgate, 2006), 218.

The result, then, is a tragic eschatology and a tragic hope. Williams' approach here has much in common with Sergius Bulgakov's conception of eschatology as a criticism of both optimism and pessimism. History, Bulgakov writes, is 'a spiritual tragedy.' There is no occasion for Christian optimism, since 'within the limits of history itself, there is no resolution of this tragedy.' But nor is pessimism admissible, since every moment of history is set against a horizon of hope. Our labour in this world 'does not tumble like a house of cards, is not destroyed by the blows of world catastrophe.' The eschatological horizon thus prevents us from absolutizing any part of our historical experience, while also investing history with a tremendous surplus of meaning. We can never possess the meaning of history, but nor can we ever assail it. It lies beyond us, in the 'metahistory' of the Pentecostal fire.[5]

Unlike more familiar varieties of Christian eschatology, this is a vision that refuses any final gratification of human desire. Insofar as it withholds ultimate consolation, it is a tragic vision. But it is tragic, I suppose, only from the perspective of unredeemed desire. To the warped neediness of selfish desire, even God's triune love seems tragic rather than the highest bliss. Once desire has relinquished fantasy, the same love appears as eschatological joy. Not because it satisfies us, but because it is infinitely more than anything that merely satisfies. What we experience as a dark night of negation is in fact the searing brightness of divine joy.

So the difficulty is to speak of Christian hope in a way that resists the incessant pull towards an idiom of self-gratification. Williams sees this difficulty – inherent to all theological discourse – with painful clarity. His scholarly prose style, so burdened with uncertainties and laborious equivocations, is often itself an expression of exactly this problem. Just as an alcoholic might try to hijack his desires by hiding the bottle, so theology must lay traps for itself in order to prevent itself from becoming a final word. Paradoxically, Williams thinks it is only by *refusing* a definite eschatological position that theology sustains its eschatological commitment, its openness to a future that is strange and unforeseen. 'A finished account of Christ as containing all meanings would

[5] Sergius Bulgakov, *The Bride of the Lamb* [1945], trans. Boris Jakim (Grand Rapids: Eerdmans, 2002), Chapter 6: 'History.'

make christology non-eschatological.'[6] Eschatology, then, is never a positive description of the end. Yet eschatological language is necessary, even essential, since it marks a limit, the point at which all our language about God comes under judgement.

This austere and reticent approach to the language of Christian hope springs from Williams' most elemental intuition: that it is Jesus who teaches us to speak of God; that the bleak landscapes of Gethsemane and Golgotha map out the strange topography of God's inner life. At the real heart of things are kenosis, crucifixion, resurrection – in other words, tragedy and its transfiguration. Christian hope is not a cosmic optimism, not a denial of tragedy. It is the vision of a lamb standing amid the ruins of history, 'looking as if it had been slain' (Rev. 5.6).

---

[6] Rowan Williams, 'The Finality of Christ' [1990], in *On Christian Theology* (Oxford: Blackwell, 2000), 94.

11

Prayer

. . . finding in the unfixable
a bizarre homeliness.[1]

'In the whole history of Catholic theology there is hardly anything that is less noticed, yet more deserving of notice, than the fact that, since the great period of Scholasticism, there have been few theologians who were saints.' That was Hans Urs von Balthasar's melancholy observation in 1948. Until the late medieval period, he says, most saints were also theologians who reproduced the church's teaching not only in ink and paper but also in the solid tissue of their lives. Their influence on the tradition came from this unity of life and teaching; their believing was also a knowing, and their knowledge was a function of their faith.[2]

If I had to point to a single text that resonates with Williams' imaginative life, it would perhaps be Augustine's *Confessions*, a work that uniquely fuses spirituality with theology. Augustine articulates truth about God by talking *to* God: the reader is an eavesdropper on his theology. That is why reading the *Confessions* is a curiously lonely experience. It is bittersweet, because for once *we* are on the outside looking in, whereas in most theological writing it is the scholars who talk among themselves while *God* is presumed to be outside. The cold modern distinction between theology and spirituality is rendered meaningless in Augustine's language of prayer. In the opening paradox of the *Confessions*, he asks whether we first pray (in order to know God) or first know God (in order to pray). How

---

[1] Rowan Williams, 'Thomas Merton: Summer 1966,' in *The Poems of Rowan Williams* (Grand Rapids: Eerdmans, 2002), 65.

[2] Hans Urs von Balthasar, 'Theology and Sanctity' [1948], in *Explorations in Theology* I (San Francisco: Ignatius, 1989).

could we call on a God whom we don't already know something about? But how could we know anything about God unless we've already prayed? Augustine never resolves the paradox. There is no need to decide whether prayer or theology takes priority. We simply find ourselves caught up in the mystery of prayer, and experience of this mystery is itself a kind of knowing. The whole *Confessions* is thus a demonstration of the mutuality of praying and knowing. The activities of spirituality and theology are integrated not by any theoretical method, but by the integrity of a sanctified life, a life that prays. That is why the *Confessions* – perhaps the pinnacle of theological writing in the western tradition – is not a systematic doctrinal treatise but an autobiography, an account of one human life swept up in the shattering tempest of divine love. Only here, in the converted life, do theology and spirituality join hands.

This conception of the spiritual life is present everywhere in Williams' work; it is the milieu of his imagination. He has poured his thoughts into this Augustinian cast just as the words of a poet are poured into the small, liberating form of the sonnet. He finds in Augustine a model of what it looks like to speak of God with integrity, so that the struggle for truthful speech becomes part of a wider pattern of devotion to God, attention to God, love of God.

Williams' work is thus animated by this Augustinian passion for the conversion of the mind to God. This is why he finds himself crossing the boundaries of so many different genres and disciplines. It is why he soon became restless with academic life at Cambridge and Oxford, and seemed driven ineluctably into the hard and unedifying business of Christian leadership, first as Bishop of Monmouth and Archbishop of Wales, then as Archbishop of Canterbury. Some people become church leaders through careerism, cunning, and political calculation. For Williams, one suspects it is more a matter of obedience, discipline, and kenosis – as well as of theological integrity.

When he published his 1991 essay on 'Theological Integrity,' many readers must have been taken by surprise.[3] In theological discourse, 'integrity' is generally used to describe the internal harmony and coherence of a theological system; but Williams disavows that sort of integrity. Instead, what interests him is the spiritual integrity of

---

[3] Rowan Williams, 'Theological Integrity' [1991], in *On Christian Theology* (Oxford: Blackwell, 2000).

theological reflection and the life that practises it, an integrity that subverts our pretensions to theological mastery or completeness. Williams accepts the postmodern critique that our language about God often conceals the interests of those who speak it. Theology easily becomes a covert exercise in gaining and keeping power. We can't overcome this tendency by a readymade theory, as though theology could pull itself up by the bootstraps and extricate itself from all power interests. Rather, Williams argues, our talk about God is really freed only when we direct our language *to* God in prayer and praise. Prayer subverts the hidden power operations of our language. For what is prayer except a confession of our own failure, our hunger, our incompleteness before God? What is prayer except a renunciation of power, giving up any 'total perspective' in order to stand expectantly before God? Prayer is the crucial thing: it is a cross for religious language. It is the means by which our speech 'articulates its own incompleteness before God,' and so 'turns away from any claim to human completeness.' And only as we turn away from the idolatrous desire to occupy a divine standpoint can genuine conversation with others begin. Conversing with God humbles us just enough to begin conversing with others. And so the stammering, hopelessly inefficient language of prayer both nourishes and judges our religious speech.

We are inclined to think of Christianity as a tradition of ideas, an elaborate system of beliefs stretched out across time. But Christian tradition is primarily and essentially a tradition of prayer. It is a millennia-long experiment in listening to God and replying to God while looking at the crucified Jesus. Christianity is the historical community in which this peculiar form of attention is cultivated. Like Balthasar, then, Williams thinks that the subject matter of theology is not only texts and traditions but also 'people who pray'[4] – lives in which speech about God has attained a degree of integrity.

This is another reason why Williams returns so often to the figures of saints, those lives that show what integrity really looks like. The separation of theology and spirituality into separate domains is a wound within faith itself, not merely a convenient division of labour; attention to prayer and sanctity is a salve for this wound.

There is a sort of sanctified folly, a glorious ineptitude, in a life devoted to prayer. Such lives are often quite marginal to the great

---

[4] Williams, 'Theological Integrity,' 13.

powers and institutions that determine the movement of history. Yet from lives such as this we learn what it really means to speak of God. If theology is an attempt to get to know God, then we will have to go to those places where God is most deeply at work: to the church's hidden history, the history of its saints, its mystics, its people of prayer. As Balthasar has said, it is the one who loves God who really knows God. And so theology has to include, as one of its raw materials, the lives of those who pray.

Christian theologians then ought not to be impassive observers or cynical experts on the language of religiosity. Knowledge of God is possible only from within, only as we find ourselves caught up in the terrible dynamism of God's life, God's love, God's giving. As the fourth-century ascetic Evagrius Ponticus said, the theologian is the one who prays, and the one who prays is a theologian.

Williams' thought here owes a great debt to Simone Weil, that unwashed, unorthodox mystic with her famished appetite for divine love. In her celebrated essay on school studies,[5] Weil describes the cultivation of 'the faculty of attention,' the opening of ourselves to what is objectively there. In this way we become supple to reality, 'penetrated by the object.' The spiritual activity of waiting produces truthful knowledge: 'We do not obtain the most precious gifts by going in search of them but by waiting for them.' Williams takes from Weil this conception of the intimate union between love and knowledge, spirituality and study. Prayer makes theological knowledge possible, and knowledge circles back again and arrives, as though for the first time, in the mystery of prayer.

For Williams, therefore, the point of theology is not to solve our puzzles or answer all our questions. Nor is it the hubristic enterprise of creating unassailable systems of thought. Theology rather is a spiritual discipline, a labour of intellectual asceticism. It is the cultivation of patient, attentive adoration of the mystery of God. Theology and spirituality meet in contemplation, where we are no longer describing God from a distance, but participating in a mystery that penetrates the whole world of human experience. We are 'questioned, stripped naked and left speechless' by a reality that we cannot control.[6]

---

[5] Simone Weil, *Waiting for God* (New York: G. P. Putnam's Sons, 1951).

[6] Rowan Williams, *The Wound of Knowledge* [1979] (2nd ed.; London: Darton, Longman & Todd, 1990), 1.

It should be clear by now that when Williams draws on traditions of negative theology, his concern is not with any general theory of the limits of language. The simplest misunderstanding would be to see here something like the semiotic apophaticism of Derrida, in which meaning is never available but always deferred. A more disturbing mistake would be to imagine that, for Williams, divine reality itself is inherently dark and uncommunicative. In fact, he thinks just the opposite: not that there is too little meaning, but that there is too much. When we pray, when we hear the words of scripture, when we celebrate the eucharist, we are saturated with meanings. God is too full, too communicative, too bright and piercing. It is God's nearness that makes God so strange, God's brightness that strikes us down as though blinded. For Williams, negative theology is not a way of coping with the poverty of human speech, but a celebration of the inexhaustible riches of divine meaning. Here, 'negative' language is a bit like the language of any friendship. In the company of a close friend I sometimes find myself reduced to silence, not because the relationship is wordless (nothing is more verbose than friendship), but because in friendship you can never say enough; the real goal of friendship is to talk your way into silence. In the same way, religious language is a language of unsaying. In prayer, speech ripens into silence. The language of theology spills over into the baffled joy of contemplation and praise.

Williams often describes religious language with one of his favourite metaphors, the mystical trope of divine darkness. The point of this paradox is not that God is inherently dark, but that God's radiance is too much for our poor eyes. We have crouched too long in darkness; when the door is flung back wide, we cringe in fright, squinting against the light. As Milton said in *Paradise Lost*, God is 'dark with excessive bright.'[7] God's brightness is our dark night; God's beauty is the vanquishing of our desire.

Williams thus thinks that Christian negative theology arises not from the limits of human knowledge, but from the very pattern of the divine life as an unceasing rhythm of kenosis. Following Vladimir Lossky, he concludes that negative theology is not a conceptual device, but is 'anchored in the reality of

---

[7] John Milton, *Paradise Lost*, 3.380.

personal kenosis.'[8] It is simply a way of saying that God is God.
The collapse of language into contemplative silence occurs
where we are exposed to the drenching downpour of God's self-
communication. Language is overwhelmed by all that God means.
It falls silent because there is too much to say, and a human life is
not large enough to contain it. Our struggle for faithful speech is
really a struggle for spiritual capacity, for lives that are spacious
and hospitable to divine truth. 'Narrow is the house of my soul:
enlarge it.'[9]

We have been tracing this same pattern throughout every
chapter of this book. Williams' theology of sociality is really
a negative picture of social life: truth emerges only in the
contradiction between lives that are irreducibly different. It is not
success that matters so much as failure, not agreement so much
as conflict, not achievement so much as patience and endurance.
In turn, human sociality rests on an infinite depth of God's own
desiring, loving, and self-giving. God's love is not an ultimate
gratification but a dynamism that surpasses every desire. Not
only to human eyes, but even within the depths of divine being,
God is 'dark with excessive bright.' This negative theology of
desire is, for Williams, the meaning of the doctrine of the trinity.
Similarly, Williams' negative theology of hope stresses that the
eschatological dimension of faith comes into view only as we
exercise an 'eschatological reserve,' refusing to take God's point
of view or to imagine that we could occupy a divine standpoint
as the interpreters of history.

Again, Williams thinks of the saint as a sort of negative definition
of humanity. What is sanctity but the dispossession of a human
self, the unwriting of a human biography? The sanctified life is not
perfect and complete. If anything, it is more elementally incomplete,
more nakedly exposed to the tragic limits of human experience. The
saint is often the furthest thing in the world from what we would
call a successful life. Over the saint there hangs not a reassuring
nimbus but a shadowy question mark. There is no solution to the
strangeness of the saint, the weakness of the saint, the madness

---

[8] Rowan Williams, 'The Deflections of Desire: Negative Theology in Trinitarian Disclosure,' in *Silence and the Word: Negative Theology and Incarnation*, ed. Oliver
Davies and Denys Turner (Cambridge: Cambridge University Press, 2002), 134.

[9] Augustine, *Confessions*, 1.5.6.

of the saint. The saint is mad with God's wisdom, broken by God's wholeness, wounded by God's unbearable nearness. This ambiguity is intimately related to the riddle of Christ: Christ the foolish wisdom of God, Christ the fragile Pantocrator, Christ the ambiguous revelation of God's brightness. As Williams says of the theology of Luther: 'God himself is the great "negative theologian," shattering all our images by addressing us in the cross of Jesus.'[10] What prayer is to speech, what difference is to sociality, what the saint is to a damaged humanity, so the cross is to the world, and so Christ is to God.

---

[10] Williams, *Wound of Knowledge*, 158.

12

Fantasy

The earth is full of masks and fetishes,
. . . He is a stranger to them all.[1]

When Karl Barth lectured on Christian doctrine, he used to begin
the semester with Feuerbach's critique of religion: he had assimilated
Feuerbach's stringent atheism right into the centre of his conviction
about what it means to speak of God. In the same way, Williams
takes Freud's critique of religion as a fundamental criterion for
language about God. Iris Murdoch has issued the solemn warning
that 'almost anything that consoles us is a fake.'[2] If Williams'
thought has any absolute criterion, it is this conviction that truth is
never merely consoling, that it has to be hard and angular, purged
of the distorting influences of the ego.

I do not think it is an exaggeration to say that a dread of self-
deceptive fantasy is, in fact, the secret engine of Williams' work. It
motivates his reformulation of the doctrine of the trinity, so that the
life of God is understood as eternally restless, eternally unsatisfied
desire. It underpins his rather brooding analysis of Christian hope
as the purgation of human desire. It lies behind his emphasis on the
hiddenness of God's work: the crazy eccentricity of the saint, for
example, is a cure for ecclesiastical fantasy. It drives him to think
of the spiritual life not as wholeness but as a sort of stripping bare,
until finally nothing remains but an absence, the hollow centre
of the human self, the dark night of desire. In short, the problem

---

[1] Rowan Williams, 'I Saw Him Standing,' translated from the Welsh of Ann Griffiths,
in *The Poems of Rowan Williams* (Grand Rapids: Eerdmans, 2002), 100.

[2] Iris Murdoch, *The Sovereignty of Good* (London: Routledge & Kegan Paul,
1970), 59.

of fantasy leads him to envisage Christian faith as one enormous pattern of asceticism and kenosis.

But where does all this talk of 'fantasy' come from? In the first instance, it owes much to Augustine's mercilessly self-critical search for that elusive thing, a truthful confession. In Augustine's view, Williams observes, 'self-knowledge is a practice of criticism, specifically the criticism of the way the subject distorts its self-perception.' Proper self-knowledge is precisely a knowledge of the limits of the self, its incompleteness and propensity to deception.[3] But Williams goes further: he fuses this Augustinian doctrine of the self with the exacting rigour of Freudian suspicion.

It is true that he seldom has a good word to say about the father of psychoanalysis – he once began a book review with the remark: 'Freud was wrong.'[4] He is frequently critical of the type of simplified Freudianism that one finds everywhere in contemporary western culture, and he is especially impatient with the crude materialism which sees all human relations as the disguised operations of blind instinct. Likewise, he gives short shrift to psychologizing interpretations of the gospel which read the story of Jesus as a dramatic projection of the inner life of the soul: 'Jesus "redefines" the human psyche, it does not define him.'[5] But such hostile references to psychoanalysis are also rather misleading. Williams has, in fact, read Freud deeply and sympathetically, and he has absorbed Freudian suspicion like a curative poison, a purgative for the Christian imagination.

His most explicit discussion of Freudian psychology appears in an encyclopaedia entry from the early 1980s.[6] The criticisms of Freud are here as stinging as ever: he speaks of Freud's 'crude scientism' and his 'painfully absurd' cultural anthropology. Yet this doesn't let religion off the hook. The central claim of Freud's critique of

---

[3] Rowan Williams, '"Know Thyself": What Kind of Injunction?' in *Philosophy, Religion and the Spiritual Life*, ed. Michael McGhee (Cambridge: Cambridge University Press, 1992).

[4] Rowan Williams, review of James Alison, *Faith beyond Resentment*, in *The Tablet* 10 November 2001.

[5] Rowan Williams, 'Interiority, Interiorization,' in *The Westminster Dictionary of Christian Theology*, ed. Alan Richardson and John Bowden (Philadelphia: Westminster, 1983), 304.

[6] The following quotations are from Rowan Williams, 'Freudian Psychology,' in *The Westminster Dictionary of Christian Theology*.

religion remains important. Freud sees religion as an attempt to cope with the tragic dimensions of human experience, by locating power and agency outside the human subject. In Williams' words:

> Religion attempts to deal with the powerlessness of the human subject; but rather than being itself a means of empowerment, it projects unrestricted power on to an alien reality and fixes the self in a permanent state of impotence and alienation. Power (divine power) is accessible only through self-abasement and self-devaluing.

In the first place, Williams responds by noting that the Christian tradition doesn't promise any human access to divine power; instead, Christians speak of God's power as the source of a radical human dependence. And recognizing our dependence on God need not be self-destructive: 'To depend for one's identity ultimately upon a hidden source of self-giving or self-sharing is to be as free as one can be within the tragic limits of the world.' Finding the source of our being beyond ourselves is not necessarily alienating but can become a doorway into freedom and self-awareness.

Yet Freud's critique – even if it misses the distinctiveness of a Christian understanding of power and subjectivity – is painfully accurate as a psychological analysis of the way we treacherously turn 'God' into an instrument of human power. It is because our hearts crave the cold familiar touch of idols that our theology stands 'in constant need of demythologizing.' Our provisional, imperfect language about dependence on God slips very easily into self-protective claims. Freud exposes the workings of this psychological machinery; he forces us to ask whether our theologies are really driven by our own fears and insecurities. Commenting on Christian belief, Freud observes:

> We say to ourselves: it would indeed be very nice if there were a God, who was both creator of the world and a benevolent providence, if there were a moral world order and a future life, but at the same time it is very odd that this is all just as we should wish it ourselves.[7]

Our speech about God is easily hijacked by our own yearnings for pleasure, security, and control; where this occurs, 'God' becomes a projection of human wishes and an instrument of human power.

---

[7] Sigmund Freud, *The Future of an Illusion* (New York: Doubleday, 1957), 53–54.

There is nothing innocent about religious fantasy: our most deeply felt needs and anxieties give birth to the monsters of idolatry. Fantasy is more than just a comforting illusion; it is a murderous hatred of reality. As Williams sees it, the business of theology is thus to unmask our fantasies, to subject our ideas about God to a searching criticism. In this way, theology anticipates the Freudian critique, exposing our dangerous longing for the comfort of false images of God.

Here Williams sees an affinity between psychoanalysis and negative theology: both function as a criticism of idols, stripping away the fantasies that protect us by imprisoning us in a false world. Psychoanalysis can press 'towards the purifications of a negative theology which is constantly suspicious of the religious temptation to seek for absolute knowledge.' Indeed, in 1983 Williams could even repeat Donald Evans' judgement that Freud is a 'master of the contemplative way.'

This appropriation of Freud reflects the influence of the British novelist and philosopher Iris Murdoch. Murdoch was another former student and close friend of Donald MacKinnon (though the friendship had abruptly ended when she portrayed MacKinnon's marriage in a novel). During his student years in the 1970s, Williams met Murdoch in Oxford, and he committed himself to a thorough study of her work. Her writing made a deep impression on him, and her austere reworking of the Freudian notion of fantasy has remained central ever since to Williams' theological vision.

Though Murdoch could not be called a 'Freudian' in any detailed sense, she argued that Freud uncovered the psychological functioning of what Christians call original sin.[8] Freud's pessimistic assessment of human nature points to where our real moral difficulties lie. He shows how hard it is for human beings to be unselfish, objective, and realistic. Goodness, Murdoch observes, 'is the almost impossible countering of a powerful egocentric mechanism.' The 'fat relentless ego' is always intent on drawing everything into its own orbit. The way we see things tends to be illusory, a projection of ourselves on to reality. Thus our own perceptions have to be met with a ruthless and exacting suspicion.

Williams follows Murdoch in all this; and he also follows her when she turns to Simone Weil's doctrine of 'attention.' Only when

---

[8] The following quotations are from Murdoch, *The Sovereignty of Good*, 46–76.

I look at something objectively, when I see what is really there, am I disabused of my selfish projections. Attention takes me beyond myself; it is contact with reality. As Murdoch writes, 'the direction of attention is, contrary to nature, outward, away from self . . . towards the great surprising variety of the world.' It is only by seeing something beyond myself that I am freed from selfish fantasy. Thus Freud has the right diagnosis but the wrong treatment. He shows that we are plagued by fantasy, but psychoanalysis only makes things worse if it draws us still further into the dismal chambers of the self. 'It is an attachment to what lies outside the fantasy mechanism, and not a scrutiny of the mechanism itself, that liberates.'

So what the selfish ego needs, Murdoch thinks, is not so much therapy as *art*. To look at a painting and perceive its sheer material otherness; to be pierced by a piece of music that cannot be assimilated into my own experience; to read a novel that exposes me to the startling fact of another human consciousness – this is what art gives us, this capacity for selfless attention. Gerard Manley Hopkins spoke of 'all things counter, original, spare, strange' – and it is such a vision of the particularity of things, the strangeness of what is really there, that overthrows our fantasies. Hence Murdoch argues that art is one of the essential sources of moral action, since it is one of the few points at which human beings deliberately cultivate a truthful seeing of reality. The objectivity of artistic creation – where a painter or poet or musician says not 'I like it' but simply 'there it is' – is a mutiny against the rule of solipsistic fantasy.

Williams' commitment to the moral importance of art likewise springs from this conception of fantasy and attention. In a study of the aesthetics of Jacques Maritain, he underscores the objectivity of artistic creation: 'Art . . . dispossesses us of our habitual perception and restores to reality a dimension that necessarily escapes our conceptuality and our control. It makes the world strange.'[9] Our normal perceptions are self-interested and self-protective; art is unsettling, unsafe, unconsoling. It is a revolt against the ego. The moral importance of poetry, for example, depends not on whether poets possess special virtues but on whether they *see* something objectively, something our own perceptions had filtered out. Poetry is a mode of exposure. In a 2006 sermon on the anniversary of the

---

[9] Rowan Williams, *Grace and Necessity: Reflections on Art and Love* (London: Continuum, 2005), 37.

birth of Shakespeare, Williams suggested that 'something is missing in the poet, some habit of self-defence that allows most of us not to know a lot of what we'd rather not know.' Poets live with a 'wound' of understanding. They are hurt by reality. They show what it takes 'to live with one's own undefendedness,' without the protective mechanism of fantasy. The poet's strength, then, is really a kind of debilitating weakness, a 'poetic lack' that renders the ego painfully susceptible to truth.[10] Poetry is ontology, as Maritain said.

And holiness, too, is ontology: a sort of lack in which a human life is exposed to the solid, strange objectivity of God. The saint, the artist, the poet – they are the eyes of the world looking back at God.

I sometimes wonder whether every serious theology is at heart an apologetic, an attempt to make the Christian faith intelligible within a changed world, and to make the world intelligible within a Christian frame of reference. Williams' later theology – all that we have been exploring in the second half of this book – is perhaps best understood along these lines. The whole direction of his later thought is towards a post-Freudian apologetic, an attempt to show that Christianity absorbs, right at its heart, the full force of Freud's critique of religion. That is why Williams responds to the problem of fantasy with a doctrine of divine desire – the doctrine of the trinity. Even the life of God resists gratification. The Son is eternally unconsoled, eternally broken, by the love of the Father; the Father is eternally devastated and displaced by the gift of his being to the receptive Son; and a third agency, the Spirit, is the constant evacuation of fantasy, a dark night poised between God and God, light and light. If tragedy means a total lack of completion and consolation, then it is hard to avoid concluding that there is something very like a tragedy going on forever between the persons of the trinity.

And in this world there can be no consolation, only a deeper descent into the purging fire of divine love. Tragedy is the ash that remains after fantasy has been burned away and the old gods have been thrown down.

---

[10] Rowan Williams, 'A Sermon for Shakespeare Sunday,' preached in Stratford-upon-Avon, 23 April 2006: http://www.archbishopofcanterbury.org/articles.php/1598/a-sermon-for-shakespeare-sunday.

13

Renunciation

So what shall we say, amazed, when the dead sun
turns inside out for morning?[1]

Williams is really just a person who has taken his imagination along
to church: that is perhaps the most important thing to be said about
him. He has tried to gather his thoughts around the pattern of
religious devotion to Christ. Yet that devotion has a particular style
and posture. Its defining feature is an austere asceticism – an almost
overwhelming horror of the power of self-deception, combined with
a vigilant alertness to opportunities for renunciation. Devotion to
Christ as ascetic renunciation of fantasy: that is the theology of
Rowan Williams.

Against the dark backdrop of selfish fantasy, we can at last fully
appreciate Williams' recurring emphasis on the strangeness and
hiddenness of Christ. What does it mean to say that God's presence
in the world is hidden? From a Romantic perspective, the divine
hiddenness might easily be understood as a temporary veil that is
pulled back in moments of sudden epiphany. Here the strangeness
of God becomes material for human manipulation, just as, in
Romanticism, nature is manipulated by techniques of self-discovery
and self-awareness. All this still leaves the selfish ego at centre stage: an
ego that seeks spiritual gratification through sudden epiphanies is still
a selfish, unredeemed ego. As Williams argues in a recent essay,[2] such

---

[1] Rowan Williams, 'Lent,' translated from the Welsh of D. Gwenallt Jones, in *Headwaters*
(Oxford: Perpetua Press, 2008).

[2] Rowan Williams, 'Divine Presence and Divine Action: Reflections in the Wake of
Nicholas Lash,' an address written for a colloquium at Durham University in June 2011:
http://www.archbishopofcanterbury.org/articles.php/2131/divine-presence-and-
divine-action-reflections-in-the-wake-of-nicholas-lash.

a Romantic conception of religious experience still rests on a faulty view of human subjectivity; it posits 'a kind of pure subjectivity which must be taught to go in search of the truth, and which finds its most satisfying object in experience of the divine.' The result is a self-serving aestheticizing of divine hiddenness: God as a flash of insight, something merely to be looked at and enjoyed, rather than an environment to be inhabited through discipline and devotion. In short, even talk of God's 'strangeness' can easily be drawn into the dark pull of human fantasy, so that once again God becomes a means of private gratification.

For Williams, the alternative to Romanticism is a ruthless Augustinian realism. Christ is a stranger because we are trapped in a world of self-deception; even when Christ appears to us, we make him a screen on which our own desires can be projected. He is, in other words, strange to us because *we* have become strangers. He seems to be hidden because *we* are hiding from truth. And we emerge from hiding not through any single moment of insight, but through holy living: the slow process, year upon year, of discovering that the self is not the centre of things, but is derivative, receptive, conditioned by an act of threefold love and giving. Communal disciplines and practices of renunciation are thus the means by which the self slowly gropes towards an awareness of its own displacement, an awareness that our labours of self-protection are no longer necessary, since human freedom is found not in a posture of anxious grasping but in receptivity and response. We find ourselves only as we begin to lose hold of ourselves, and so become free to receive ourselves as a gift. It is here, then, not in momentary epiphanies but in the habitual environment of holy living, that we discover human identity as the 'site' of God's identity: that is the point of Augustine's trinitarian theology, and it is, for Williams, the whole solution to the Freudian problem of fantasy. It is the holy life that cracks open the hard shell of the ego 'by making for me in the world the room I thought I had to conquer and possess.'[3]

In all this, Williams wants to show that redemption is possible in spite of the tragic brokenness of human experience; that a generous, expansive social life is possible in spite of the shrunken immaturity of the self; that love is possible in spite of the ego, with its elaborate

---

[3] Rowan Williams, '"Know Thyself": What Kind of Injunction?' in *Philosophy, Religion and the Spiritual Life*, ed. Michael McGhee (Cambridge: Cambridge University Press, 1992, 226).

apparatus of selfish projection. The whole of his later theology is, in other words, an apologetic recovery of the Christian meaning of the word *love*. For 'God is love; and those who dwell in love dwell in God, and God dwells in them' (1 Jn 4.16). Freud was right to argue that religion springs from unwholesome desire: but God is the criticism of desire, because God is love.

It is, ultimately, the love of God that teaches us to tell the truth about ourselves. In his recent lectures on C. S. Lewis' Chronicles of Narnia,[4] Williams speaks of 'our inability to tell our own stories truthfully,' so that 'we have to be told our stories in the presence of love.' Only then, through God's loving word of truth, are the layers of self-deception peeled away. And as Williams also says in these lectures, the opposite of redemptive love is the nightmare of ego-centred fantasy. We all end up with what we most deeply desire. If what I ultimately desire is myself, that is just what I will get: it is called hell. That's what Milton's Lucifer discovered, that hell is not an external environment but the small interior wasteland of the self: 'Which way I fly is hell, myself am hell.'[5]

Williams' theology then is a subtle, elegant, and imaginative response to the challenge of Freudian suspicion – but it comes at a price. In order to answer the Freudian critique, he necessarily retains the scaffolding of Freud's bleak – his almost unbearably tragic – vision of humanity. Within these limits, redemption can be pictured only as the slow expansion of the self towards others, a sort of widening spiral in which the self allows the lives of others to become its own centre. If this process were ever to cease, it would mean the self had again become fixed, stable, turned inwards. And so failure and incompleteness – or to put it positively, patience and growth – are the real heartbeat of Williams' imagination. He has recovered the meaning of the word 'love,' but the price he pays is one that I have mentioned many times throughout this book: it is tragedy.

Williams' theology is a precarious attempt to walk the tightrope between these two points, tragedy and love. Arms flung wide, occasionally flailing, he makes his way along the wire, never

[4] Rowan Williams, 2011 Holy Week Lectures: http://www.archbishopofcanterbury. org/articles.php/1703/archbishop-of-canterbury-discusses-narnia-in-holy-week-lectures.

[5] John Milton, *Paradise Lost*, 4.75.

daring to rest for long at any one point – for as anybody knows who has ever tried to walk a tightrope, the main thing is to keep moving. It is the same tightrope that T. S. Eliot traverses in the *Four Quartets*, consumed as he is by the ineluctable alternative between two fires:

> The only hope, or else despair
> Lies in the choice of pyre or pyre –
> To be redeemed from fire by fire.

The cost of Williams' achievement is a sort of pervasive ontological sadness: to see all things coloured by a tragedy older than the world. It is no momentary sorrow, but a deep conviction that life must always remain unconsoled, that the best we can hope for is to be stripped bare, exposed, and forgiven under the stark relentless light of reality. That is what it costs for him to utter, in a post-Freudian world, 'the shrill sentence: God is love.'[6]

Is it not true here, above all, that Williams remains 'Orthodox in an Anglican form'? The deepest patterns of his thought, I suspect, are drawn from the piety of Russian Orthodoxy, with its tendency to elevate extreme examples of monastic renunciation as the truest form of devotion to Christ. Indeed the problem of fantasy is also embedded in traditions of Orthodox piety, most notably in the hesychastic practice of mental asceticism through silent prayer. Readers of the *Philokalia* will recall the constant refrain concerning the dangers of spiritual delusion (*prelast*), together with the appeal to wakeful attention as a means of combating falsehood. Is it any coincidence that Williams' own piety is built on this daily practice of mental asceticism?[7]

Then again, we should remember that Williams is also very much a *Welsh* thinker. Compare him for a moment to Dewi Sant, the sixth-century patron saint of Wales: barefoot, clad in skins, clenching a stick, living on wild leeks, relentlessly mordant in his mysticism, penitently reciting scripture while standing up to his neck in

---

[6] R. S. Thomas, 'On the Farm,' in *The Bread of Truth* (London: Hart-Davis, 1963).

[7] The hesychastic practice involves techniques of breathing combined with silent repetition of the Jesus Prayer ('Lord Jesus Christ, Son of God, have mercy on me'), often
with the use of a prayer rope for counting. Williams has often spoken of the foundational role of this practice in his daily piety.

ice-cold lake water. Williams is an intellectual ascetic: he has clothed his thought in skins like John the Baptist.

Perhaps the best way to characterize Williams' thought is, finally, to say that it is a theology of preparation. It resembles nothing so much as the forty days of Lent: a theology of slowness and discipline, abstinence and privation, the 'luminous sorrow' of the great fast.[8] His uniqueness as a thinker lies in the unflinching severity with which he submits his imagination to the ascetic dimensions of Christian devotion. Yet the pattern of Christian devotion is more than renunciation. It is feasting as well as fasting, absolution as well as confession, the oil of gladness as well as ashes of mourning. In the Christian year, the famished asceticism of Lent gives way at last to the joyous feast of Easter; the brooding solemnity of renunciation dissolves into the self-forgetfulness of psalms of praise and benediction; the fire of purgation becomes a Pentecostal flame. A theology of Lent is a great thing: but one cannot live by ash alone.

Still, we should remember that this Lenten theology is intended as a Christian response to Williams' own time and place, just as much as Barth's 'theology of crisis' was a response to the nineteenth-century ideology of progress, or as Moltmann's 'theology of hope' was a response to the crippling despair of post-war Europe. For western societies today, consigned to a slow death by the poison of a ruthless and decadent self-centredness, there is perhaps nothing we more urgently need to hear than Williams' mournful Lenten strains, his call to the hard preparatory work of fasting, renunciation, and dispossession.

---

[8] That is Sergius Bulgakov's description of Lent in *Churchly Joy* [1938], trans. Boris Jakim (Grand Rapids: Eerdmans, 2008).

14

Writing

Not to make sense but room.[1]

In Herman Melville's *Moby-Dick* – that sprawling great tragic novelization of Milton and *King Lear* – the narrator describes his own story as an unfinished work, partial and imperfect just because it is 'grand' and 'true.' 'God keep me from ever completing anything,' he declaims.[2] There are religious orders in which a vow of silence is observed; Williams has taken the Melvillean vow of incompleteness. It is, he thinks, better to grow than to finish.

And Williams' importance for contemporary thought lies not only in his ideas but in the *way* he engages the tradition – especially the way he writes. His writing is patient, delicately exploratory, moving between genres, languages, and idioms with a teeming, inquiring restlessness. He is, like Augustine, 'one of those who write as they progress and progress as they write.'[3] Even his most accomplished works have about them a fragmentary quality, something reluctant and retiring. Williams is not the sort of writer who wants the last word. For a writer so preoccupied with the search for truthfulness, he is, in fact, surprisingly reticent about bringing truth directly into view. As a writer, he is like the persona in George Herbert's 'Love III,' approaching not confidently but with shy pauses and averted eyes. His theology is not so much an orderly arrangement of themes as an assemblage of discrete textual performances, a written ensemble, a

---

[1] Rowan Williams, 'Thomas Merton: Summer 1966,' in *The Poems of Rowan Williams* (Grand Rapids: Eerdmans, 2002), 65.

[2] Herman Melville, *Moby-Dick* (Evanston and Chicago: Northwestern-Newberry, 1988), 145.

[3] Augustine, *Epistle* 143.2.

disparate set of experiments with the imaginative possibilities of a living spiritual tradition.

The plasticity of the Christian tradition is evident in these diverse experiments with theological language. Not that his writing is always successful, but in its many different genres and idioms it is always aiming for the same thing: a sort of contemplative wakefulness, a capacity to see. Writing, for Williams, is not so much a means of communicating ideas as a spiritual discipline and a mode of attention. Indeed, he has compared the difficulties of writing with the difficulties of holy living. Writing is hard because it forces us to confront our fantasies and illusions; it is an exercise in truthful seeing, and that is always a hard thing. 'The bit we have to discard in our writing is what we think is best – which is often what most easily fits our expectations . . . . We need to develop a ruthless eye for hidden weaknesses, to make things difficult for ourselves as we write.'[4] That is why writing is so hard: in order to make any progress, I have to learn hard things about myself. Indeed the real difficulties of writing are not technical but spiritual: behind every paragraph the selfish ego lies in ambush. Failings in language are at root spiritual failings.

Readers have often complained of the laboured syntactic complexities of Williams' scholarly writing, and it is a fair complaint. The essays collected in On Christian Theology, for instance, are at times unduly ponderous, their laboured paragraphs crammed full of qualifications and self-conscious hesitations, their arguments tending to draw back from the bracing clarity of precise conclusions. Yet this has to be set alongside Williams' unusual commitment to the generous labour of translation (from Russian, French, German, and Welsh);[5] his historical research, which refracts the light of tradition into the present in surprising new ways; his devotional writings, where modest inviting sentences and homely imagery become instruments for probing the riddles of ordinary

---

[4] Rowan Williams, Silence and Honey Cakes: The Wisdom of the Desert (Oxford: Lion, 2003), 68.

[5] His translation work is substantial: Pierre Pascal, The Religion of the Russian People (Crestwood, NY: St Vladimir's Seminary Press, 1976) (from French); Hans Urs von Balthasar, The Glory of the Lord, Volumes 3, 4, and 5 (Edinburgh: T&T Clark, 1986, 1989, 1991) (from German, as co-translator); Sergius Bulgakov, Sergii Bulgakov: Towards a Russian Political Theology (Edinburgh: T&T Clark, 1999) (from Russian); as well as many poems translated from Welsh, Russian, and German.

human experience; his literary criticism, where the writer's language yields to the gentle pressure of other voices, other imaginations, even other theologies; and, finally, his poetry, where considerations of self-expression and didactic utility are suspended before the simple joy of *making*, of doing new things with words. If Williams is a difficult writer, it is also important to remember that poetry is *par excellence* the language of difficulty: its one aim is to overcome the deceptive, deadening familiarity of language, to make language as strange as it needs to be.

Taken together, this profusion of styles and genres points to what might be called a catholic theology of writing. Every piece of writing, like all the varied stuff of human experience, can nudge our speech a little closer towards truthfulness, and so towards God and one another.

It is one of the casualties of academic culture that theologians today tend to give so little consideration to their own use of language. When the conventions of academic discourse become self-legitimating, we can easily begin to assume that *how* we talk about God is relatively unproblematic, the only real question being *what* we say. The result is a sort of linguistic Docetism that tears apart form and content. Williams is alert to this dangerous heresy, since he is persuaded that Christ remains a stranger even (or especially) to the language we use to describe him – a stranger, then, also to those curious specialized language-games represented by the institutions of church and academy. How does one speak of a reality that is both native and foreign to human culture and human language? Once this question has been raised, the practice of writing is drawn into the substantive theological problem of christology.

If Christ is a stranger, then our attempts to speak of him will be fraught with peculiar difficulties. How can we speak of a stranger without eventually turning him into something familiar? What forms of speech can best help us to relate to Christ's uncanny nearness? Williams responds to these questions not with a comprehensive theory of language, but by *writing*, by entering into a process in which human speech gropes towards the strange, solid reality of Christ.

Williams was widely criticized when, amid the deepening Anglican crisis in 2007, he withdrew to spend three months in the United States, writing a book on the fiction of Dostoevsky. Critics assumed, no doubt, a straightforward contradiction between exercising

Christian leadership and spending a quiet summer reading Russian novels. But one could read his Dostoevsky book as an argument for the affinity between the creation of fiction and the creation of faithful Christian community. Iris Murdoch has described the creation of fictional characters as a mode of love: 'Love is the perception of individuals. Love is the extremely difficult realization that something other than oneself is real.'[6] Thus as one literary critic has observed, 'there is nothing harder than the creation of fictional character.'[7] The writer of fiction withdraws from herself, suspending her own agenda with such intense attention that another personality is allowed to come into being. So the practice of writing is a sort of slow, excruciating kenosis of the self. You write not in order to assert what you already know, but to open yourself to what is still strange and unfamiliar. Sarah Coakley has described the Christian life as a 'willed effacement to a gentle omnipotence.'[8] Isn't writing just such an act of disciplined self-effacement? Isn't it just the kind of generous selflessness that is the true mark of Christian sociality? As though what the church needs most in a time of crisis is not better techniques of leadership and management but an enlarged capacity to listen and to see. As though reading a Russian novel might be the most appropriate, the most profoundly serious, response to a communion torn apart by self-interested rivalries.

In his preface to *David Copperfield*, Charles Dickens spoke of the sorrow with which he brought his fictional characters into being. 'An author feels as if he were dismissing some portion of himself into the shadowy world, when a crowd of the creatures of his brain are going from him for ever.' For Williams, the theological significance of fiction lies in this dimension, the way novels allow other human selves to exist. Writers of fiction do not project themselves on to the page but withdraw, circumscribing their own personalities in an enormous exercise of self-restriction. The novelist, Williams says, undertakes 'a self-emptying in respect of the characters of the fiction, a degree of powerlessness in relation to them.' Authors are morally bound to refuse a degree of control over their narratives,

---

[6] Iris Murdoch, 'The Sublime and the Good,' in *Existentialists and Mystics: Writings on Philosophy and Literature* (London: Chatto & Windus, 1997), 215.

[7] James Wood, *How Fiction Works* (London: Jonathan Cape, 2008), 75.

[8] Sarah Coakley, 'Kenosis and Subversion,' in *Powers and Submission* (Oxford: Black-well, 2002), 37.

so that the characters can be fully and ambiguously human. Writers cannot have the last word even over their own creations;[9] they love their characters enough to let them be. And this 'letting be' is of course never passive but an act of intense personal involvement and commitment: it is love. Here human authorship becomes analogous to the divine authorship of humanity. God's creative labour does not imprison us but gives us real freedom and moral integrity. Thus Williams suggests that the doctrine of the incarnate Christ is 'the cornerstone of a theory of the novel.'[10]

This theology of writing is a sort of abridgment of all Williams' thought on God and language. And it provides an intriguing window on to his own practice of writing – that colourful panoply of styles, languages, idioms, and genres; that painstakingly crafted oddness; that arresting imaginative vitality; as well as the failures, the collapses into awkwardness, the clumsy hesitations, the brooding self-awareness which is sometimes too visible and too pronounced.

Perhaps Williams' most serious failing as a writer lies in the relentlessness with which he reads Christian texts, causing him at times to overwhelm the real differences of another position by the sheer force of his own vision. There is a striking example of this tendency in a 1979 essay on Karl Barth, where he tries to align Barth with a kenotic picture of the trinity.[11] Williams argues that, in Barth's theology, God risks the divine identity in 'the inconceivable self-emptying' of the crucifixion. The divine being contains a 'gulf of contradiction and opposition,' so that God's act in Christ 'incorporates in itself the extremest possible risk of its own failure and deficiency.' This is an unusual interpretation of Barth, though one in which Williams' own commitments are immediately discernible. The whole reading is, in fact, based on a single passage from Barth, which Williams quotes at length:

It therefore pleased [God] . . . for the redemption of the world, . . . to deny the immutability of his being, his divine nature, to be in discontinuity with himself, to be against himself, to set himself

---

[9] Rowan Williams, *Dostoevsky: Language, Faith, and Fiction* (Waco: Baylor University Press, 2008), 137, 234.

[10] Williams, *Dostoevsky*, 61.

[11] Rowan Williams, 'Barth on the Triune God' [1979], in *Wrestling with Angels*, ed. Mike Higton (Grand Rapids: Eerdmans, 2007), especially 129–36.

in self-contradiction . . ., in this inner and outer antithesis to
himself.

The only problem is that this passage has nothing to do with
Barth's understanding of the trinity. It is, in fact, the summary of an
'alternative' position which Barth promptly proceeds to reject. On
the same page, after summarizing this kenotic view, he condemns
it as 'an image of our own unreconciled humanity projected into
deity,' and even as a 'supreme blasphemy.'[12] In Williams' essay,
however, Barth's description of this 'alternative' view is lifted out
of context and made the foundation of a thoroughgoing kenotic
interpretation of the trinity. It is an egregious interpretive mistake,
though also an understandable one. In his eagerness to find a place
for contradiction and kenosis in Barth's thought, Williams fixes
immediately upon a passage that shows him just what he wanted to
see – and so he neglects to go on reading to the end of the page. A
simple mistake, then, but also a revealing one. Williams is already
deeply committed to a particular vision, and he is too quick to align
Barth's thought with his own theological outlook. His own prior
commitment to tragedy, negativity, and kenosis becomes a sort of
filter, so that an important (in this case, the *most* important) detail
in Barth's text becomes invisible.

A similar process of filtration might account for that remarkable
distinctiveness of Williams' readings of diverse parts of the Christian
tradition. In the 1970s, wherever he turns he seems to find traces
of tragedy and kenosis. In that decade, there is surprisingly little
difference between his readings of T. S. Eliot, Martin Luther,
and a Russian thinker like Vladimir Lossky. Similarly, after his
great discovery of Hegel in the early 1990s, there is an uncanny
uniformity of vision across a very diverse spectrum of scholarly
studies, so that his interpretations of Augustine and Hans Urs von
Balthasar can seem all but indistinguishable from his close readings
of Hegel. More recently, in his attention to the doctrine of the
trinity, Williams' intricate and sympathetic readings of Augustine,
Thomas Aquinas, and John of the Cross seem also like a seamless
interpretive garment. And isn't Williams' deep preoccupation with
the problem of fantasy in danger of becoming myopic? When even

---

[12] Karl Barth, *Church Dogmatics* IV/1 (London: T&T Clark, 2009), 184–85.

the four Gospels are interpreted as prescriptions against fantasy,[13] one gets the feeling that 'fantasy' has become a key that unlocks every door – and that Christ's story has been interpreted in light of this idea, instead of vice versa. It is clear that Williams has an aversion to 'total perspectives' and comprehensive systems: but does he protest too much?

To be sure, Williams' imaginative power lies in this same relentlessness of vision, the capacity to pursue his own questions through even the darkest labyrinthine passageways of Christian tradition. But the single-mindedness of the pursuit can become a blinder, so that important dimensions of the tradition disappear from his field of vision. Perhaps that is why his theology, so intensely focused on renunciation, can seem at once so compelling and so unsettling. Nevertheless, if writing is a mode of exposure to truth, then even failure can be exemplary. After all, it was Williams himself who said that the best theology is like the noise of someone falling over things in the dark.

The Russian iconographer Leonid Ouspensky has described the strangeness of the visual language of icons:

> The strange and unusual character of the icon is the same as that of the Gospel. For the Gospel is a true challenge to every order, to all the wisdom of the world . . . . The Gospel calls us to life in Christ; the icon represents this life. This is why it sometimes uses irregular and shocking forms, just as holiness sometimes tolerates extreme forms which seem like madness in the eyes of the world, such as the holiness of the fools in Christ . . . . Madness for the sake of Christ and the sometimes provocative forms of icons express the same evangelical reality. Such an evangelical perspective inverts that of the world. The universe shown to us by the icon is one which is ruled not by rational categories or by human standards, but by divine grace.[14]

Does not all Williams' writing make sense if we think of it as an attempt to cultivate this iconic dimension? In his demanding,

---

[13] Rowan Williams, *Christ on Trial: How the Gospel Unsettles Our Judgement* (London: Fount, 2000).

[14] Leonid Ouspensky, *Theology of the Icon*, trans. Anthony Gythiel (Crestwood, NY: St Vladimir's Seminary Press, 1992), I, 191–92.

sometimes disturbing, explorations of Christian language, we are meant to glimpse a world whose perspectives are strangely skewed. Even when Williams' writing is hard and angular, even when it is unnecessarily slow and laboured, even when it catches like a bone in the throat, it is because the writer is trying to make room for something else, something strange, solid, original, something near and hard to grasp.

And this is a *catholic* view of writing, since speaking of God does not require any specialized esoteric idiom, as though God were inaccessible to the mundane dimensions of our experience. Every use of language can be a venture for truth and a denial of fantasy. The work of writers is to piece back together some of the brittle glass of ordinary human experience, to assemble little windows through which the world looks at God and God looks back at the world.

Writing, then, is a spiritual exercise. Its whole aim is to become supple and receptive, yielding gently to the strangeness of the one who is quietly and subversively at work in our words, ploughing the dark furrows of our language, sowing in our speech the seeds of a new world.

EPILOGUE

Some years ago, I remember taking an afternoon walk down the quiet suburban street where my wife and I were living at the time. It was early summer, and a warm breeze stirred the languid jacarandas that bloomed beneath the canopy of cloudless Queensland sky. After rambling about for some time, I noticed a woman walking towards me from the far end of the street. I had left my glasses at home, as I often do when I am out for a stroll, but even at this distance I could make out the curve of her hips and the dark tresses falling about her shoulders. A long skirt swayed as she walked, and I could see that she was carrying a baby at her side. I had never seen her before: I knew I would have remembered her. Perhaps she was new to the neighbourhood? Though I am by nature a shy person, on this occasion I decided I would pause a moment and speak to this lovely apparition as she passed me on the street. I would catch her eye and smile, welcome her to the neighbourhood, ask where she was from, perhaps make some innocent flirtatious remark. I kept watching her figure as she drew nearer, my thoughts lulled by the jacaranda breeze and the easy rhythm of her hips. And then, with a delighted disorienting shock, I saw – what I would have seen at once had I been wearing my glasses – that the splendid stranger was my wife, walking in the sun with our baby daughter on her hip. 'You were with me, and I was not with you,' writes Augustine in the *Confessions*. The one I knew best was the most alluring stranger, veiled in sunlight. Not that she was hidden, but that I was. And in that simultaneous shock of illusion and truth, blindness and sight, my wandering desire for the lovely form of a woman was ambushed by the woman I love. 'You were radiant and resplendent, and you put to flight my blindness.'[1]

There is another story about a splendid stranger on a road: the story of Christ on the way to Emmaus. I have said that Rowan

---

[1] Augustine, *Confessions*, 10.27.38.

Williams' work is a Lenten theology: and so it is. But his thought might also be read as a decades-long, multifaceted meditation on the Emmaus story. All the unwieldy complexity of his work comes into focus around that still point. All his painstaking experiments with language form a kaleidoscope, focused always on the same christological centre – a centre that morphs into new shapes and colours with each successive turn of the tube.

In the story, the two disciples are pondering Jesus' death as they make their way down the road. And amid their melancholy theological discussion, the risen one himself joins them and begins to talk with them along the way. 'But their eyes were kept from recognizing him' (Lk. 24.16). His identity is a secret. Even when he opens the scriptures to them, they fail to see him. Only with the breaking of the bread are their eyes opened. For one startling moment they recognize him: but at that moment the elusive stranger slips away once more.

Williams retells the story in a recent poem, 'Emmaus' (2008).[2] As we make our way towards Emmaus, we experience an alteration of perspective, barely perceptible. The lines of light and shadow seem subtly different, our faces and voices strange to one another. Then without warning the stranger is with us on the road:

First the sun, then the shadow,
so that I screw my eyes to see
my friend's face, and its lines seem
different, and the voice shakes in the hot air.
Out of the rising white dust, feet
tread a shape, and, out of step,
another flat sound, stamped between voice
and ears, dancing in the gaps, and dodging
where words and feet do not fall.

The stranger is completely out of step with our familiar world. He walks to a different rhythm, padding in the gaps between our uncertain footsteps. His voice is syncopated, entering our conversation only in the gaps, dodging into those small clipped silences between our words. It is disconcerting, and we don't know how to respond. It is as though language itself were coming apart:

---

[2] Rowan Williams, 'Emmaus,' in *Headwaters* (Oxford: Perpetua Press, 2008), 21.

When our eyes meet, I see bewilderment
(like mine); we cannot learn
the rhythm we are asked to walk,
and what we hear is not each other.
Between us is filled up, the silence
is filled up, lines of our hands
and faces pushed into shape
by the solid stranger, and the static
breaks up our waves like dropped stones.

The stranger on the road is an awkward presence, like an inarticulate dinner guest who reduces everything to a clumsy stammering. The familiar rhythms of our speech are distorted by his syncopation. We no longer understand one another: he is cramming his words into the gaps, creating a heavy 'static' that thwarts our attempts to communicate. It is a sort of auditory claustrophobia, in which every silence seems too full. The stranger has pressed himself into the human distance between us; he is uncomfortably close, pressing hard against our language and our lives, pushing us out of shape – or rather 'into shape' – by his stifling nearness. His weight presses down on us, paralyzing our speech.

But as the poem concludes, we recover our language at last in the breaking of bread:

So it is necessary to carry him with us,
cupped between hands and profiles,
so that the table is filled up, and as
the food is set and the first wine splashes,
a solid thumb and finger tear the thunderous
grey bread. Now it is cold, even indoors,
and the light falls sharply on our bones;
the rain breathes out hard, dust blackens,
and our released voices shine with water.

The 'solid stranger' on the road is now recognized in the 'solid thumb and finger' that serve the eucharistic bread. We had been walking at dusk, and our faces were concealed in shadows. But now we see one another clearly. Christ is risen: our lives are washed in the clean light of his rising. Everything we ever said about God is broken on Christ: in him everything is given back and made new.

This stranger, whom we know so well, has loosened our captive tongues. He bursts our levees, surging through us like a flood. There is no need to hide anymore, no need to protect ourselves from *him*. Now everything is simple, as plain as bread on the table. Outside the dark clouds are lowering, the ground is black with rain. But inside, in the cold dark, our faces shine, our voices are quick and bright with the joyful articulacy of praise.

AUTHOR INDEX

SUBJECT INDEX